TRAPPED IN MY SPORTS BRA
AND
OTHER HARROWING TALES

by

Marlene Kern Fischer

TELEMACHUS PRESS

COVER AND INTERIOR ART AND DESIGN BY DANIELLE CLEMONS

Photographs used with permission

Publishing Services by Telemachus Press, LLC
7652 Sawmill Road, Suite 304
Dublin, Ohio 43016
http://www.telemachuspress.com

ISBN: 978-1-956867-26-8 (eBook)
ISBN: 978-1-956867-27-5 (paperback)

HUMOR / Family and Relationships
Version 2022.04.21

What readers are saying about Marlene Kern Fischer's book,

GAINED A DAUGHTER BUT NEARLY LOST MY MIND: HOW I PLANNED A BACKYARD WEDDING DURING A PANDEMIC

I follow Marlene Kern Fischer's blog on Facebook—*Thoughts from Aisle 4*. I knew about the wedding, the dilemmas and the outcomes. Even so, I absolutely loved the book! Marlene reminds me so much of Erma Bombeck! Her writing flows from her pen as if she is speaking out loud. Kudos, Marlene! I look forward to the next one!

—Bob

It did my heart good to read this book. I've enjoyed the journey of keeping traditions and coping with this crazy pandemic! Very great read! Thanks for sharing.

—Debbie

Really funny and clever story of pandemic woes. This author is a real mood elevator.

—Eileen

Charmingly witty and authentic!

A quick must-read for anyone who wants to be reminded of the joy in the simple, yet most important things that life can offer us: love, health, family, friends, tradition, and Phish. Mazel Tov!

—Dee

Pandemically inspired, literary sunshine!

I couldn't love this book more! This sweet-and-true story, moved along by wit, humor and the musings of a loving mom, makes this book a true treasure.

I can envision it becoming a bestseller. Not only is it a joy to read, I think this book is the perfect gift for any mother of the bride/groom, past, present and future. It's tenderness and love wrapped up in hilarity. I gave it five stars, because that's the highest score on Amazon. I'd give it more stars if I could.

—Sissy

To purchase your copy of *Gained a Daughter But Nearly Lost My Mind: How I Planned a Backyard Wedding During a Pandemic*, visit your favorite online retailer.

You can follow Marlene's blog ,*Thoughts From Aisle 4,* on Facebook or find her on Instagram @aisle4Marlene

ACKNOWLEDGEMENTS

First, I'd like to thank my husband Mark (to whom I sometimes refer as Mr. Aisle 4) for his constant encouragement, love, and support. His edits make my writing better, as well as grammatically correct.

I'd also like to thank all my kids, original and add-ons, for giving me such awesome material to write about and allowing me to tell their stories.

A few more thank yous:

Thank you, Helene Wingens, for your objectivity, literary acumen, and continued encouragement.

Thank you, Danielle Clemons, for enhancing my books with your amazing artwork.

Thank you, Diane Schwemm, for inviting me to write for CollegiateParent six years ago, for helping edit this book, and for believing in me.

Thank you, Deb Notis, for your comments and suggestions. It's been fun talking books with you.

Thank you, Rachel Berson, for catching all my mistakes.

Thank you to all my friends and family who are my cheering squad. I appreciate you more than you know.

Thank you to the local shop owners who sold my first book in their stores. Shout out to DeCiccos, Beginnings Bleus, Tazza, Town Center Pharmacy, Luxe, and Sammy's. David Perlow: Those two last books you bought made all the difference. (I'm not kidding.)

Thank you to Dr. Maureen Empfield for helping me through my mental health crisis. If you are struggling, don't be ashamed to talk about it or seek help. You are not alone.

And last but certainly not least, thank you to all my *Thoughts From Aisle 4* readers for helping me publish this book and for making Aisle 4 such a wonderful community. You restore my faith in humanity daily.

INTRODUCTION

When I was a teenager, I loved Erma Bombeck. I assume most of you have heard of Erma Bombeck, but for those who haven't, she was a writer and newspaper columnist. She also wrote many books with long titles like *If Life Is a Bowl of Cherries, What Am I Doing in the Pits?*, *The Grass is Always Greener Over the Septic Tank*, and *When You Look Like Your Passport Photo It's Time to Go Home.*

Erma wrote about her kids and husband—she was basically one of the first bloggers. And she was funny. Laugh out loud funny. What struck me most was her honesty and irreverence. I grew up in a household where being irreverent was not encouraged.

I have no idea why a teenage girl would relate to a grown woman's existence. But I did.

I desperately wanted to be Erma. Someone who could tell stories about everyday stuff and make people laugh. Erma could also be serious and poignant. I wanted to be that, too.

Erma taught me that things don't have to be perfect. And we don't have to pretend our lives are something they are not. No one has perfect kids.

Okay, perhaps some kids are better behaved than others, and they might APPEAR to be more perfect. But I can almost guarantee that they have some weird behavior their parents aren't telling you about.

I did do some writing. But then... Life happened. And I got busy raising my three sons. My writing fell by the wayside.

For a long while, I forgot about Erma. But when my sons were mostly grown and needed me less, I began writing again. Turns out it's never too late to remember your dreams.

One of my first published pieces, *Confessions of a Blogger*, appeared in the *Erma Bombeck Writers' Workshop*. To have my name linked with Erma's in any way gave me a sense of utter joy and a feeling of accomplishment. I had that piece framed and it hangs in my bedroom. I've also had the honor of being one of the judges of an Erma Bombeck writing contest.

When one of my readers tells me that I remind them a little bit of Erma Bombeck, I feel like I've been paid the highest compliment.

Thank you, Erma, for leading the way.

A friend asked me what this book is about and I told her, "Life." Although I tried to put the stories into categories, there is no overall arc that connects them other than the fact that they all are true. Except perhaps for the satirical pieces (which probably have *some* truth to them).

Like Erma, I've written about what I know best—parenting, love, loss and growing older. I have to say that the parenting stories are much more fun from the "remember when" perspective, as opposed to living through them in real time when I thought I might possibly not survive and I didn't know how things would turn out.

I hope you enjoy *Trapped in My Sports Bra and Other Harrowing Tales* as much as I enjoyed writing it.

XO, Marlene

TABLE OF CONTENTS

TRAPPED IN MY SPORTS BRA
AND
OTHER HARROWING TALES

I want my children to be
independent thinkers.
Except when I tell them
what to do.

~Thoughts From Aisle 4

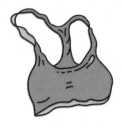

1. PARENTING—THE GOOD, THE BAD, AND THE UGLY

THE TALE OF THE RED PENS

Some children are compliant. Their report cards always say things like "a pleasure to have in class." Conferences with their teachers tend to be glowing and complimentary. When you finish speaking with them, you want to skip out of the classroom, go home and hug your child and then congratulate yourself on having raised such an amazing person.

Well, my oldest son wasn't one of those kids. Let me get one thing out of the way—it wasn't the academics that was the problem. He generally had that area covered. He just got annoyed easily by the teachers and other students and in turn annoyed them back.

Perhaps balking at the rules was a hobby or a sport to him, perhaps it was hard for him to conform all the time—I never was exactly sure what was going on. Younger teachers tried to find ways to motivate him to behave: coupons for extra computer time if he would sit still, extra assignments to keep him busy, etc. The older teachers tended to have less patience; several even retired shortly after having him in their class. Some years were worse than others. There was one particular year in middle school that was the worst of all.

Fairly early on in seventh grade, I started getting weekly phone calls from my son's science teacher. She said my son was disorganized and was lying on the floor during class—my son said he was kneeling to get some papers out of a binder. The teacher said he didn't raise his hand and was calling out. My son said she didn't see him raise his hand. On and on it went until I started having stomach pains whenever I saw the school's number come up on my phone.

I told my son to knock it off because I was going to have a nervous breakdown. The teacher requested a conference with us, so my husband and I went in to speak with her and the rest of the teachers on my son's team. Most of the other teachers didn't seem to have a problem with my son—this was primarily a battle between him and the science teacher.

The teacher asked me if my son had an "organic disorder." I later figured out that this was code for asking me if he had ADHD and if perhaps he had meds he could take before her class. We took him to a neuropsychologist who tested him and said he was bright and motivated. She assured us that he would be a productive member of society, which I was greatly relieved to hear.

We opted not to medicate him—it's not that I don't believe in medication; I do. But I also feel that when a student is successful academically, albeit not completely compliant, medication may not be warranted.

Three quarters through the school year, I got yet another call from the teacher. This time she told me my son was not using the required red pens in class. I assured her I would get to the bottom of the matter. I asked my son why he wasn't using the red pens as he had been instructed. He told me he had been using a red PENCIL because he didn't have any red pens. Apparently, he had lent his red pens to other students, and he thought he might have lost some as well. He was somewhat vague about the specifics.

Having reached the breaking point, I went to the store and purchased red pens. A LOT of red pens. I told my son he had better use those red pens and give the extra cases to the teacher for any student who did not have a red pen in class that year or the year after (and for years to come). Thankfully, I never heard from her again.

Years later, the principal of the school would remind me of the tale of the red pens whenever I saw him— he called my handling of the matter "creative problem solving." When my youngest son had the same teacher ten years later, I told him to keep a low profile and hoped she had forgotten about us. I told the principal I was too old for any more

shenanigans. Fortunately my youngest son is more of a rule follower.

My oldest son graduated from middle school, high school, and college. The calls from the teachers (and professors) eventually stopped. Six years ago he graduated law school and in 2020 married his college girlfriend whom we love.

So the next time you have school conferences, if you have a child who isn't always "a pleasure to have in class," don't be discouraged. Be consistent, but don't give up or lose faith. They will get there—and you may look back and remember your own red pens story and smile.

MAKING YOUR LIFE A MASTERPIECE—AN ADOPTION STORY

For the past twenty-five plus years I have been fielding questions and comments regarding my son's adoption. The first time it happened I was grocery shopping with my baby when a man standing in front of me said, "Now you will get pregnant." I looked behind me to see if he was addressing someone else and when I saw no one, I realized he was talking to me. I must have given him a quizzical look because he elaborated, "Now that you've adopted, you will get pregnant. It happens all the time."

A little flustered, and in no mood to discuss my fertility with a stranger in the produce aisle, I responded that my baby was the spitting image of my husband and walked away. I generally am open and honest about things, but people, there is a time and place for certain discussions.

That may have been the first but it was certainly not the last time I had to address the issue. When my son was in kindergarten, his teacher called me up to tell me that on St. Patrick's Day, he had told the class that his birth father was Irish, a story she was certain he had fabricated. I pointed out that the term "birth father" was sophisticated language for a five-year-old and, in fact, his story was true.

I also told her that I knew of two other adopted children in the class. Now this was completely false, but I thought trying to figure out which children were the adopted ones would keep her busy for a while—perhaps even too busy to call me again. (You'd be correct if you'd gotten the sense that I didn't enjoy hearing from teachers.)

As my son grew (and grew and grew), it became even more apparent that he did not physically resemble us. When I am out with my son, people look at the two of us and ask me "Is your husband tall?" I am 5'4" and my son is over 6'1" so I guess it's a logical question. But when I reply that no, my husband is not tall, the questions continue.

At this point I should mention that my son is half Thai (and very handsome, I must add). You'd think people would be able to put two and two together, but that's usually not the case. If I tell people he was adopted, the questions often continue. I have been asked what country he is from. Unless Florida has seceded from the Union, I am pretty sure he was born in the United States. My son works at the company where my husband also is employed and when he first started, he was amused when people assumed his dad was the Information Technology guy rather than the General Counsel. I won't even comment about stereotyping.

Then there is the ultimate adoption reflection. People have expressed their doubts to me about whether they would be able to love an adopted child as much as they do their biological child. To those people, I have responded with a question of my own. "What if you discovered there had been a mix-up at the hospital and the child you brought home was not genetically linked to you—would you love them any less?" Of course not.

Love is about familiarity and commitment, the intertwining of lives, not about a genetic connection. Adoption is the term for what happens on the day you get your child; parenthood is the term for what happens every day after that.

A friend of mine who was adopted once told me that your "real" mother is the one who causes you to need psychotherapy. Perhaps that's true. Despite my mistakes, I hope my three sons know that I love them with all my heart and always have their backs. I hope they hear my (cautionary) voice in their heads before they do something dumb and know how proud I am when they do their best.

It's only fair to mention that in addition to the personal, amusing, and odd comments we have heard over the years, there have been incredibly positive sentiments. A card we received after we brought our son home said, "Sometimes you need to color outside the lines to make your life a masterpiece."

We colored outside the lines to help us create our family and the result is beautiful.

I THINK MY SON IS A CIA OPERATIVE

I hope this doesn't blow his cover...

It took me a while to figure out that my youngest son is in the CIA.

I'm not sure when they recruited him—possibly as early as elementary school. That's about when he stopped talking. I don't mean that he went mute; he just stopped sharing details. About everything. Maybe at that point he was just practicing for his future career in the CIA. I'm not sure how young their trainees are.

As he got older, all the other moms in his friend group seemed to know what was going on with the kids. Except me of course. Little things, big things; I knew nothing. They would assume I had heard that the kids were going to a ballgame or the movies. But, if I didn't hear it from them, I didn't hear it. It was a little embarrassing at times.

Occasionally, the CIA lifted my son's ban on sharing, and I would get some small nugget of information which I cherished like gold.

By the time my son started college he was an advanced CIA operative. He claims to be a math major but who really knows? It's entirely possible the math thing is just a cover. Or maybe he's taking college classes while he's working for the CIA. That would make sense since the university he allegedly attends sends us a tuition bill every semester.

Last spring I discovered that he'd been dating a girl. For six months. Which is a long time to not mention you've been seeing someone. We found out accidentally through one of his brothers.

Youngest son does call home a fair amount. More often, in fact, than his older brothers did when they were in college. And I appreciate that a lot because I love hearing his voice. When he calls, I have to frequently check to make sure we haven't been disconnected and he's still on the line. Because there's a lot of dead silence. I do my best to carry the conversation but eventually I run out of questions, and we say goodbye.

Here's a typical conversation:

Me: How's it going?
Him: Good

Me: What's new?
Him: Nothing

Me: Get any grades?
Him: No. (apparently there are no grades ever at this school he attends)

Me: How are you feeling?
Him: Fine

Me: Anything else to report?
Him:

Me: Are you still there?
Him: Yeah

Me: Okay. Thanks for calling, Love you.
Him: Love you too.

By the way, he does mention when he needs money. Apparently the CIA doesn't pay that well or my son has an off-shore bank account we don't know about.

My CIA boy's girlfriend is definitely NOT in the CIA, and we have actual conversations where she uses words and fills in a lot of blanks. When I first met her, I had a ton of questions. I was a little worried I'd scare her off but luckily it hasn't happened.

For the record, it's not like my older boys tell me everything. They most certainly do not. I'm on a need-to-know basis, which means they tell me what THEY think I should know. But they wouldn't qualify for the CIA.

And that's okay because one CIA operative in the family is enough.

A LETTER TO A YOUNGER ME FROM AN OLDER ME

Now that I'm on the other side of parenting (meaning my three sons are mostly grown and I'm no longer in the trenches), I've had some time to reflect. When I say reflect, I mean think about things I think I got right and things about which I was off base. There are things I wish I had known—things I would tell my younger self about being a mother if I could. Here is some of what I would say...

Dear Younger Me,

First:

I am not going to tell you to enjoy every minute of parenthood because, if I offer that advice, I know you will find a way to reach across time, into the future, and smack me (and you would also think an impostor was writing to you). While one kid is vomiting and another is shrieking and the third is out of sight and up to who knows what, it's hard to think about how fleeting time is. I realize that from where you're standing right now, time may as well be standing still. Just know that the time will pass and, despite their best efforts to break you, you will survive mostly intact.

Give them your all but:

Save a little something for yourself. I threw myself into parenting because it's the job I always wanted. However, I wish I had done just a tiny bit more for myself. Like writing—I know I barely had time to think, much less create cogent and insightful sentences, but I wish I had held tighter onto the things that were important to me. I'm grateful to get a chance to do more now but I wish I hadn't waited so long. So, younger me, please listen and nurture yourself, as well as those children. Carve out a little time for you.

Stop worrying so much:

I understand you can't help worrying. Unfortunately, that's not going to change in the future. But I can tell you that all the worrying you are doing is a huge waste of time and effort. At least try and dial it down a notch if you can. Or start meditating a little so you can be a tiny bit more Zen.

You're not screwing them up:

Good news: despite a few mistakes we made along the way, they all turned out fine. They are pretty hardy and resilient creatures. Even the high strung one. In fact, they are more than just fine—they are terrific. They aren't necessarily tidier, but they are good people who care about each other, their friends, and their significant others. Yes, they ALL have significant others. They are now human enough to have partners—nice ones you're going to like. You will finally have other females in your life. And, as a bonus, I want you to know the kids will be able to get jobs and support themselves.

It's just a phase:

The baby who wakes up all the time? He does learn to sleep through the night. And that kid who only eats pasta? He will start eating chicken, steak, and veggies at some point. How about the one who keeps having tantrums and throws things when he loses? Yup, he will stop doing that. In fact, he's so docile now it's hard to believe he's the same person.

And how about the one who can't manage his money? Okay—we're still working on that one, but I'm guessing he'll learn how to do it someday soon. My point is, although their personalities don't completely change, most of the behavioral stuff really is just a phase. Just ride it out like you would a wave and know that some weird new behavior will come along before you know it.

You already know this but:

Despite the craziness and lack of money and time, work on keeping the marriage magic going. Try and go out a little more; the kids will be fine without you. I know you want to be with them, but they really will grow up and have their own lives. You need to make sure you and the hubby still have things to say to each other after they are gone.

I don't want to tell you everything that is going to happen – some of it is amazing and some, well... you will get through the bad things too. And at the end of the day you will even still have a sense of humor.

Most of all I want you to know two things:

You did a great job and I'm proud of you. When it's all said and done you will be so glad you did it. So hang in there. I'll check in on you again and, if you need me, feel free to reach out and I will be there for you.

Love,
Older Me

**My favorite
child is the one
who's annoying
me the least.**

~Thoughts From Aisle 4

A LETTER TO MY SONS

I recently was reflecting on my relationship with my sons and came to the realization that there are a few things I wish would change.

For the most part, I have a strong and close bond with my three boys. However, I admit that I am somewhat unsatisfied with the communication aspect of our relationship and, since they are not shy about pointing out which parenting mistakes they think I have made, I feel I too can comment on ways in which they might improve their behavior.

Here is an open letter to my young men. I hope they read it in the spirit in which it was intended.

Dear Son(s),

I realize and accept that you are sons and not daughters. I truly am grateful that I was blessed to have you and I have never yearned for a female child. I also understand that you are not going to text or call me every hour on the hour as many of my friends' daughters do.

[Note: At this point, a reader will comment how HER son does call and text all the time which is awesome for them but definitely not the norm. To this day, my mother talks about how I told her so much while my brother was less forthcoming with details, to which I respond, "Imagine that!"]

I don't crave daily contact with you (although I wouldn't reject it). Nor do I need to know every thought that pops into your head or what you are wearing at any given moment. However, could you work on providing me with just a little more information? Like the time you got into college, and I had to hear about it from a friend? Not acceptable. And when your good friend (who I know fairly well) got engaged and YOU DIDN'T TELL ME? Stuff like that hurts my feelings. Especially when your girlfriend tells me that even *her* mother knew about that engagement. I happen to like your friends and want to know what's up with them.

I'm not asking for a lot. Just a few scraps every now and again would suffice. I know you aren't withholding information on purpose, but perhaps when something noteworthy happens, you could ask yourself, "Would Mom be interested in knowing this?" And then err on the side of over-informing, because even when I'm not interested, I'm interested, with the following caveat.

Do you realize that when you do get in touch with me, it's generally about money or to complain about something, such as your health? Let me remind you of the time you said you had a lump on your back and, after googling it, felt pretty sure you would need surgery. After texting everyone I knew to find you a doctor in the city, I waited anxiously by the phone for hours while you had your consultation. I called when I assumed you were done with the appointment and scheduling your surgery. When I finally reached you at work, you said, "Oh, it was nothing."

I was relieved but also wanted to kill you. You can't get me all worried and then not let me know everything is okay. I don't mind hearing that you don't feel well or that there's a problem, but could you also let me know when things are alright? Or when you are feeling happy? That would make me very happy. And yes, I realize it's not about me. However, occasionally, maybe it could be a little bit about me.

Oh, and another thing you seem to love talking about, but I don't really like listening to, is "how unfairly you were treated in comparison to your brothers." Here's the holy truth about parenting: Unless you are an only child there will always be some situational inequality. But in the end, it all evens out and each of you will have (pretty much) gotten what you needed. I don't have favorites—well, that's not completely accurate. Like most parents, I tend to favor whichever one of you is annoying me least at the moment.

I'll admit that as you've gotten older, things have improved. I know you love me, and I am grateful that I can count on you when I need you. You seem to view me more as a person now and I really appreciate that. We went through a lot to get to this point, and I don't want to be greedy, but I think that we can still do better.

I hope you'll take my suggestions under advisement. I'll be checking my texts to see what is new with you.

Love, Mom

THIS IS WHY TEENS FIND THEIR MOMS ANNOYING

A while back, I was stuck in traffic on a long drive with my oldest son who is now 30 and we started talking about mothers. His mother, my mother, and mothers in general. I know that my sons find me annoying at times and I accept that it goes with the mom territory.

But my son wanted me to know that it's not just me. So, since he is a person who likes visual aids, he explained it this way:

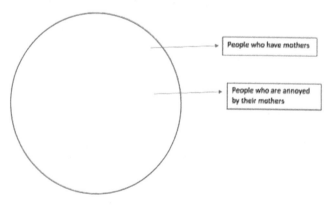

Now that we have established that all people get annoyed by their mothers, the big question is why?

My son said that he thinks that the number one reason people find their moms annoying is because we meddle. Speaking for himself (and apparently every person who has ever had a mother), he expounded on his theory by saying: "You didn't trust me to do things, but you should have because I never went so far off the path." He concluded with the following statement, which he delivered a little triumphantly: "At this point I'm out of your reach."

I heard my son out and, having a mother of my own, I didn't completely disagree with him, but I found a few significant flaws with his analysis. Contrary to his belief, parenting IS about meddling. While my son suggested that "strategic meddling" is the best tactic, when you're a parent THERE IS NO SUCH THING.

If they screw up, we know they are going to blame us, and we are going to blame ourselves. How are we supposed to know whether they are going to stray far off the path? There were times I was fairly certain my kids didn't even know where the path was. So, I believe it's best to err on the side of over-meddling. And as for being out of my reach, I will allow my dear son to think what he wants but it's just not so. My superpower is my influence, which reaches far and wide, probably from beyond the grave.

Once I ascertained why my own child found me annoying, I became curious as to why others find their mothers annoying. I posed the question to several people I know. And everyone I spoke with was more than happy to throw their mom under the bus. Even my mother, who revered my grandmother and never ever said a bad word about her, admitted that her mom could be stubborn and recounted a battle of wills between them over shoes.

My nephew said another reason moms can be annoying is their lack of filter. When asked for an example he cited a recent instance when he told his mother where his new apartment was located, and she blurted out, "Isn't that where a murder occurred not too long ago?"

When it comes to our children, our concern sometimes gets in the way of our best behavior. We have no time to pussyfoot around, so we just put it out there. That's the thing about the mother/child relationship—you don't always have to be polite.

My nephew's girlfriend was eager to join in the conversation and added that dealing with parents and technology can be annoying. And frustrating. Which I also understand—I get irritated by my own relationship with technology, so I can see how it could irritate my kids. (By the way, my youngest son helped me with that circle diagram.)

Someone else told me that her mother thinks she knows everything. Well, duh. We have a whole lot more life experience than our kids (except for that technology thing) and who better to share all that knowledge with than our children? And even if we don't know everything, we want to arm them with as much information as possible. Which is why we send them article after article even though, as my son once pointed out, they rarely read them.

In the movie *French Kiss*, when asked by Meg Ryan's character Kate if he had ever been in love, Luc (played by Kevin Kline) answers, "I loved my mother." To which Kate wisely replies, "Everyone loves their mother; even people who hate their mothers love their mothers." And even people who are annoyed by their mothers love their mothers.

I know that no matter how much I annoy my sons, they will always love me. I also know that as long as there are mothers and children, the circle of annoyance will continue.

STRANGER DANGER

The other day I had just pulled into a parking space outside the grocery store when a woman knocked on my window and indicated that she wanted me to roll it down. She looked harmless enough, so I did.

I had just called my youngest son, who's a junior in college in Waltham, Massachusetts, to discuss his rent money so he was on speaker phone when this happened.

The woman had seen the college sticker on my car's back window and wanted to know who attended the school. I told her that my youngest was there and that my middle son and his fiancée as well as my husband and I were alumni. All excited, she told me that her daughter had gone there and graduated in 2016 and was still in the Boston area getting a graduate degree. She told me her daughter had been on the swim team, loved the school, and had made such good friends. I told her that I was still very close with the friends I had made at school.

We chatted for a few more moments and she ended with an enthusiastic cheer for the school.

I rolled up my window and returned to the conversation with my son.

Me: You heard all that, right?
Him: Yeah.
Me: You're pretty horrified right now. (That was more of a statement than a question.)
Him: Yeah.

I knew this was my son's worst nightmare. I had spoken with a stranger. Anytime I had ever tried to interact with anyone when I was with my sons, they became agitated.

Them: Why are you talking to that person?????
Me: I was just being friendly. Making conversation. That's what people do.
Them: No it isn't. You're crazy.

But in this instance, someone else was initiating the conversation. So apparently I'm not the only crazy person out there.

This woman, this stranger in a parking lot, went out of her way to make a connection. And I thought it was lovely.

But in my son's mind, this was an unnecessary communication. One which involved way too many words. I think I spent more time talking to the woman than I did him.

I'm glad that my son heard the conversation. Partly to affirm that other people behave as oddly as

I do, and partly so that he could see that sometimes a random conversation can be a really nice thing.

SIX THINGS YOU SHOULD KNOW ABOUT HAVING GROWN SONS

I've read a lot about what it's like to have little boys. As a mother of three sons, I can attest to the fact that they are certainly interesting creatures. Indeed, there is much to say about them—how they love mud puddles and wreaking havoc. Their boundless energy and love of games and all things that involve balls. How snuggly they are. What it's like to clean up after them and feed them and love them and figure out how their brains work.

But what happens after those little boys grow up? Since my sons are grown now, here are six things I think you should know.

When your son grows up...

1. He won't communicate more.

Of course, there always are some exceptions. However, most boys don't feel the need to convey the trivialities of life and that will continue. There won't be constant texts and calls from him. And when you do hear from your son, don't expect him to tell you every detail of his life.

However, once in a while, when you least expect it, he may share some specifics with you. Learn to expect short answers to your questions, like "fine" and "pretty good." It's up to you to fill in the blanks around those answers. For the most part go under the assumption that no news is good news.

2. He still will make a mess.

When your young adult son comes home, even though he has been living on his own, his bed will remain unmade, his aim in the bathroom will not have improved, and you will still find dishes in or near the sink and not the dishwasher. Although annoying, you will be so happy to have him home again you will be more willing to deal with the disorder and untidiness. Because now you realize how temporary it is.

3. He still will enjoy games that involve balls.

But now his love and passion for sports will have progressed to a new level. He won't just be kicking a soccer ball in the backyard or throwing a basketball repeatedly into a plastic hoop while you marvel at his perseverance. He will watch sports on television. He will attend sporting events. He will read about sports. He will play sports. He will talk about sports with his friends. He will participate in fantasy leagues and spend time working on his draft picks and teams. He will have sports coursing through his veins. And that will not change.

4. He still will be cuddly.

When your son is home, he will appreciate a kiss goodnight (even though he's probably going to sleep later than you) as much as he did when he was a boy. And he still will be sweet. You will hear, "I love you, Mom" in a voice that, although deeper, is as earnest as it was decades earlier. When my boys were little, I always gave them a kiss after they got a haircut and told them how handsome they looked.

To this day, if one of my sons gets a haircut when he's home, he'll seek me out, point to his cheek and ask me for a "haircut kiss." Young men are more sentimental than you may realize and the traditions you create with them will endure.

5. You will be able to count on him.

Those little boys become men you can depend on when you need to. When my father died, my sons stepped up to the plate with chores and support in ways I could not have anticipated, and I felt comforted by their presence and love. I sometimes ask them for advice and their opinions on a variety of subjects. Expect that your son's shoulders will broaden, both literally and figuratively.

6. He will bring home someone else for you to love!

My sons have brought home wonderful girls whose company I really enjoy. A bonus is that the girlfriend/ fiancée/wife are better communicators than my boys (please refer back to number 1) and provide details and information about loads of topics!

When I was a little girl, I remember hearing the adage, "A son's a son until he takes a wife, a daughter is a daughter all of her life." Even back then I thought that was an odd saying and I felt sorry for the person who thought it up. Because it's just not true. So, feel free to cross that one off your long list of things to worry about.

Both my father and brother were devoted sons their entire lives and I already see that quality in my boys as well. While I occasionally miss those little boys who once dashed through the house, I truly am grateful that those boys have grown into fine men who make me proud in so many ways.

THE JOB I ALWAYS WANTED

It's amazing how one of my favorite days of the year was also once one of the unhappiest days of my life.

I will never forget Mother's Day 1990, which fell about a month after my first baby died. My husband and I were away; I had booked a trip to a tropical destination foolishly thinking I could escape my sadness. However, not long after we arrived, I discovered there was no getting away from the pervasive grief I felt. The joyous first Mother's Day I had 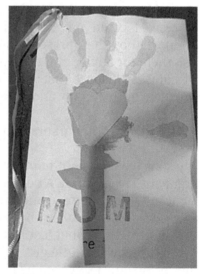 anticipated was sorrow-filled and we returned home from our trip earlier than planned.

I always wanted to be a mother. Plain and simple. The dolls I played with as a little girl were not just toys to me, they were practice for the babies I knew I would have someday. My desire for children was one of the few things of which I was certain.

Of course, there were other things I wanted to be as well: a writer, a journalist, perhaps an editor. I imagined myself working at a newspaper or in television and chose English as my major in college because I loved all things literary (except the Old English course I took). When my professors spoke, I felt like a plant getting sunlight and I tackled each reading and writing assignment with enthusiasm. I still feel that way when I write.

I would like to say my career aspirations equaled my desire to be a mother. I would like to say that because it sounds better and probably is more acceptable to say that. But if I am to be honest, although I assumed that I could somehow do it all, I knew that if I had to choose, motherhood would win out, hands down.

I remember going out with another couple we knew from college after we were all newly married. When the discussion turned to having children, my girlfriend said that, although she wanted kids at some point, she was in no rush. I told her I was in a rush, that I couldn't wait. I had no idea why. It just was something I felt compelled to do.

It was probably good that I got an early jump on things because it took a while to have those children I always wanted. There were starts and stops along the way. In addition to losing an infant, my long journey to motherhood included infertility, adoption, and, finally, joyful unexpected fertility, which resulted in my last son. In the end it took more than twelve years to complete my family. Had I started later, I might have run out of time.

The death of my first baby, along with my husband's crazy demanding career, added to the reasons I decided to become a stay-at-home mother. When I finally had a baby to bring home, I could not imagine entrusting him to anyone else. I barely could leave him for a short amount of time for fear something bad would happen. And it was not just fear; I wanted to be with him. My obstetrician, who delivered my first two babies, warned me to not be overprotective of my son. He told me this as he was performing my second C-section—I told him he could just leave the umbilical cord attached which made him laugh as he finished stitching me up.

Over the years I tried to heed his words, but it was always difficult for me. My naturally anxious nature was reinforced by that early loss. I worried about a lot of things, perhaps hoping that worrying would prevent bad things from happening. My grandmother used to tell me, "You don't know what to worry about." She was right; the things I worried about weren't usually the things I *should've* been worried about. I was generally blindsided by calamity, as most of us are. But even though I knew that, I kept worrying.

I must admit that motherhood wasn't exactly what I expected. In fact, it often was far from it. The three boys I was blessed with were nothing like the dolls I had played with as a little girl. My sons were boisterous and non-stop, and their minds seemed wired in ways I couldn't always understand.

Sometimes, like when my boys were in their pajamas and we were snuggled in bed reading together, motherhood felt like I had always imagined it would. But even on the worst days, and there were plenty of them, when they were so bad or sick and I couldn't figure out how I would make it to bedtime, never mind getting them grown up, I never regretted having them. Not for one minute or one second.

On every single Mother's Day since that first awful one I have woken up thankful that I am a mother. The special breakfast, cards, flowers, and gifts I get are all sweet and appreciated but just having my boys is enough (and if they are home, it's a bonus). I am grateful I have the job I always wanted.

"ARE YOU GOING TO TRY FOR A GIRL?"

For many years, when I was out with my sons, someone would look at them and ask me, "Are you going to try for a girl?" It happened more times than I can count.

Usually I would just smile, shake my head, and say, "No."

I had a much longer answer in my head.

First, when I was asked this question, I was past the age when it was likely I would conceive so it seemed kind of silly.

Second, after three sons, the odds of my having a girl were statistically less than the 48 percent at which I started before I had any children. So it was possible I would have to have a lot more kids before "getting" a girl. Were they suggesting that I keep going until it happened? What if I ended up with ten sons and then a daughter? Yikes! Honestly, my hands were more than full with my boys and another child of any gender would've pushed me over the brink of sanity.

Third, and most importantly, I learned early on that gender does not matter. Not even a little bit.

Before I had my first child, I imagined I would have a son and then a daughter. That was the makeup of my family of origin and for some reason I just assumed it was what I would have. If all went well, and I was so inclined, I would consider a third child.

My first baby was indeed a son. But that's where my "plan" went off course. Way off course. My beautiful nine-pound son was born with a heart defect and passed away ten days after birth. If nothing else, I am quite capable of learning from life's lessons, and this was a huge one. After that, all that mattered was bringing home a healthy child.

Forever after when I would hear someone prefer a gender I would cringe. I still do. I want to tell them my cautionary tale. But of course I don't because I don't want people to inch away from me in horror. Plus I doubt I would change any one's mind; some life lessons need to be experienced.

I was keenly aware of how extremely fortunate I was to have those three sons of mine after that initial tragedy.

When I was pregnant with my last son, I assumed it would be a boy. We all did. In fact, when we told my oldest son he would be a big brother again, he cried with happiness and said, "We will name him Isaac, because that name means laughter." And so, we did.

When I'm lonely for a little female conversation I call or text a female friend. Or my oldest son's wife, my middle son's fiancée, or my youngest son's girlfriend. And it's all good. In fact, it's more than good. It's perfect.

Sometimes now people look at me and my boys and say, "Perhaps you'll have a granddaughter." What I want to say to them is that it will matter not a single bit to me. All that matters is that they are whole.

But I just smile and nod my head and say, "Maybe I will."

DON'T BLINK

"Don't blink... just like that you're six years old and you take a nap, and you wake up and you're twenty-five... Don't blink, life goes by faster than you think."
                    Don't Blink, written by Kenny Chesney

Dear Son,

I hadn't heard that song since your high school graduation, but I heard it today when I stopped in town for an iced tea. I started thinking about our first trip out to the Midwest to look at what was your leading choice for college. Although you'd already been accepted, we hadn't seen the school yet. I wanted to see for myself whether it was the right college for you, so even though I hate to fly, off you and I went. When we were walking around the campus, I thought of all the hopes I had for you for those four years. I guess I was thinking about what I was looking for in a college for you.

I hoped you would make good friends—some of whom might last a lifetime. I hoped you would become more compassionate, mature, and considerate of others and less impulsive. I hoped your temper would mellow and that you could learn to accept losing graciously. I hoped you would improve your housekeeping skills. I hoped you would be with people who were like-minded and that you'd learn from those who weren't. I hoped you would experience romantic love. I hoped you would find a major that interested you and that you would figure out what the next step in your life would be.

Through all of it, it was my hope that you would stay connected to us. In retrospect, it was a tall order but by the end of the trip, I think we both felt comfortable that this school would be a good place for you. Not that you might not have accomplished all those things elsewhere, but we both were pleased with what we saw and felt during that trip.

Now, even though the song said not to blink, we blinked and, quite miraculously, the bill came for the cap and gown. All of those hopes I had for you have been realized to a greater or lesser degree (okay, maybe you can still use a little work on the housekeeping skills).

Your transcript and diploma reflect only a small part of what you have achieved during your four years of college. I couldn't ask for more. At graduation this week, I'll savor the moment, but only for a moment, because I have more hopes and dreams for you. And I've already started working on that list.

Love you,
Mom

THE TIME MY SON CALLED THE COPS ON US

When my middle son was around eight or nine, he called the cops on us. For real. Our crime? Not allowing him to go to a sleepover.

I was never a fan of overnights for a variety of reasons. Mostly because the kids didn't actually sleep and were hugely cranky the next day, which then became my problem. And there was the time my youngest got lice at a sleepover. Yes, I realize you can get lice anywhere but the memory of that has scarred me to this day.

Getting back to my middle son. He requested the sleepover on a night before we were to host an evening holiday meal and celebration. Since I knew we would all be up late the next night, I said "no," which made my usually docile son go a little crazy. He stormed out of the house and railed at the fates on our driveway, actually beseeching G-d to help him overcome the adversity that had befallen him. I watched for a moment, somewhat bemused, and then decided to ignore him as I went upstairs to go to the bathroom.

Next thing I know, my husband tells me I need to get out of the bathroom because a policeman was in our garage waiting to talk to us. I was like "Seriously?!" So, I went downstairs to see what was up. (I need to write about how moms don't get left alone even when they are in the bathroom; however, that's a piece for another day.

Apparently, after I left the scene of our crime, my son came inside the house and dialed 9-1-1. To be fair, my husband had put the idea in his head when he joked that our son call the police about our "abuse," a suggestion my son took seriously. Here's a tip: be careful what you say to your children as they may not always be able to detect sarcasm.

As my son started to dial, he most certainly pressed the 9 and, possibly, the first 1 before my husband took the receiver out of his hand and hung up the phone. Evidently, the 9-1-1 system is sophisticated and can detect when people *start* to dial that sequence to alert the police even without the person dialing all three digits. Or at least that's what the police officer told my husband. The officer explained to my husband that, since a call to 9-1-1 is by definition an emergency, the system tries to detect any initiation of the sequence in case whatever crisis is occurring prevents you from punching one or two of the digits.

As my husband and I stood nearby, our son proceeded to tell the police officer what we had done. To his credit, the officer listened politely for a minute or two to his tale of woe before he cut off our son. He then looked around our garage and pointed out the sports equipment, which included tennis racquets, soccer balls, baseballs, footballs and basketballs, bats, gloves and an array of cleats, bicycles and more and said to our son, "Looks like you have it pretty good here, kid."

At that point, it started to dawn on our child that he was alone in his conviction that we needed to be arrested and he was not going to get any sympathy from law enforcement. Probably suspecting that he might be the one in trouble, he stopped talking and started to look a little nervous as he stared up at the very large, no-nonsense police officer.

After their conversation, the officer left in his cruiser, and we had a long talk with our child about when was the correct time to use 9-1-1. And I had a conversation with my husband about when it's appropriate to "joke around" with our children.

We knew we would laugh about the incident someday. However that day was still a bit into the future. Like 16 years later when I was writing a book.

Although there were times with my three sons when a few days in a prison cell sounded like an excellent alternative to being at home with them, none of them ever dialed 9-1-1 on us again. We all learned a few lessons from that 9-1-1 call, including me, who decided that it would be okay to allow an occasional sleepover.

A NOTE FROM MOM

The summer before my oldest son left for college, he seemed on a mission to make sure we didn't miss him. Although he had never been an easy child, the time leading up to his departure was particularly contentious and I pretty much was counting down the days until he was gone. I've since learned that this is not a unique situation, and many parents and children find their relationships strained in the months leading up to college.

I knew that there were things I wanted to say to my son and advice I wanted to impart. However, I was pretty sure he wouldn't listen. Since I am better with the written word, I sat down and wrote him a letter. Thus began the tradition of sending my sons off to school each year with a note from me.

That first letter detailed my hopes for my son as he embarked on his college career as well as typical mom recommendations: get enough sleep, don't procrastinate, be respectful of women, etc. Knowing his strengths and weaknesses so well, I tailored that letter to include everything I could think of—it was the kitchen sink of advice notes. I hoped that he could read between the lines, which basically said, "I love you, I love you, I love you. Please come back to me in one piece." When he found and read the letter, he called and thanked me.

The next year I sent another note; based on his freshman year performance I had some further encouraging (as well as admonishing) words for my son. I told him how we hoped to hear from him more than we had the year before and that, if he had his eye on graduate school, he would need to work harder. The note was shorter than the one I'd sent the previous year. In fact, as the years went on, I discovered I had less and less to say to him. He was growing up and doing a fine job of figuring things out.

I continued the tradition through his law school years, something I hadn't remembered until I mentioned those notes to my son. By then, the letters basically were reminders to do his laundry before he ran out of underwear and clean his apartment once in a while. As always, I told him how incredibly proud I was of him. When we visited him at school, he was wearing a bathing suit because he had indeed run out of underwear and his apartment was dirty. But he was happy, had made a few great friends, and his grades were good. What more could I ask for?

When I sent my second son off to college five years after his brother, he too got a handwritten letter. His note had some of the same recommendations I'd given his brother, but there were also many different ones since he is a very different person. I tried to make the letter long enough to include all the things I wanted to say yet short enough to ensure he wouldn't get bored halfway through it and toss it in the garbage.

I reminded him to take his allergy medications and, even though he had a girlfriend, to go out and not just stay in his room FaceTiming with her. Once again, I made an impassioned plea for communication, either through phone calls, texts, or smoke signals. (I'm not all that difficult to please.)

Once again, when my youngest son left for school, I wrote him a letter that included some advice about putting himself out there socially, as well as studying without the distraction of watching sports on his devices. I already knew how difficult it is to find the exact right words, the ones which might make a difference. In the end I suppose it's less about what I say and more about having them know I was (and always am) thinking about them.

Not much in the way of material items came home with my oldest son from college; he pretty much had destroyed or lost most of the stuff we'd purchased four years earlier. He did bring home his Tempurpedic pillow and... those notes. I was deeply touched to discover he'd saved every single one of the letters I had written to him. In fact, I tear up just thinking about it. I guess they meant as much to him as they did to me.

My oldest son is now a full adult with a job and a wife. I don't write him letters anymore, but I do still offer words of advice and encouragement. I know that even when he refuses to acknowledge my advice, he's listening.

THE BIG BOOK OF PARENTING

When my kids were much younger and I would make an unpopular decision, I would tell them I needed to do it because it was in the parenting book I had been given by the hospital when they were born. I would even cite a specific chapter.

Of course we all know that, although there are many parenting books out there, there is no one definitive *How to Raise Your Kids* book. No parenting bible with a New Testament or Old Testament.

There are many times I wished that such a thing existed to help me with situations for which I was wholly unprepared. But kids are all so different and there are so many variables that even a 20-volume encyclopedia couldn't cover it all. A lot of it is on-the-job training and then being retrained for subsequent children.

I remember being out shopping with my oldest son when he was a preschooler and he decided to lie down on the floor in the store. I don't think he was tired—I just think it was a form of protest, civil disobedience because he didn't like shopping.

He ended up getting tar on his clothes that even my laundry skills could not remove. He, of course, blamed me, saying I had never told him not to lay down in stores. It's true, I had not. But I also told him I'd never explained to him not to lick toilets, which he seemed to understand intuitively.

That's the thing. There's just so much for us to know and so much we are supposed to be teaching them that it's overwhelming. We can't cover every situation. And in many cases, it's a moving target. Like how to put our babies to sleep in their cribs. My oldest son had bumpers—a big no-no now. And blankets. And I put him down on his stomach. Yikes. Going by today's standards his crib was a death trap.

By my next son, I learned that I was supposed to put him on his back and blankets were out. By my last son, we had a wedge so he could sleep on his side, and we zipped him into a cocoon-like blanket so he couldn't suffocate from free floating covers. I'm not entirely sure what they do now with babies—perhaps suspend them over the crib in a hammock-like security net that's attached to a spit that rotates them a quarter turn every 15 minutes?

Parenting takes a lot of flexibility, mental fortitude, and stamina. Having little ones is merely basic training for the teenage years. But there is no boot camp or classes that can adequately prepare you for the emotional roller coaster that is the teen years. You just jump in the ocean and do your best not to drown. Or drown your kids.

That *Big Book of Parenting* that I might have wished for probably would hold a gazillion terabytes of information, including things like how to mend a broken heart and how to motivate a child to do their best. I would have liked it to have advice on where to find patience when my reserves were gone, new ideas on what to prepare for dinner that wouldn't garner complaints, how to make sure they flushed and put down the toilet seat, how to ensure they made good choices, and, most importantly, how to learn to let go of those people I love with all my soul.

Judging by the way my kids are turning out, maybe I didn't need to rely on a book. Maybe like Luke Skywalker in *Star Wars* the (parenting) force was in me the entire time. Maybe it's in all of us. It's fine to seek advice but I believe that the best rule of thumb is to follow your instincts. You know your kids and yourself best. What works for one child and one family won't necessarily work for you. There is no correct algorithm.

And it's important to know that no one gets it all right. In the history of parenting, there has never been a perfect one. Just loving them completely for who they are will get you through. You don't need internet parenting forums or *Parenting for Dummies*. You are all you need.

WHAT KIND OF PARENT ARE YOU?

Last weekend my friend drove seven hours round trip to have lunch with her son at college. It was his birthday, but even still, I was amazed. Because honestly, it's not something I would do, and I told her that. She told me that I was a good mom too and that I did other things to make my kids feel loved and special.

I started thinking about that.

I'm definitely not one of those moms who loves to bake with their kids. In fact, I hate all things kitchen related. The fact that my sons have culinary abilities astounds me; they can cook despite me, not because of me.

When my kids were younger, I was not the mom who loved to host sleepovers. Although I did (and still do) enjoy having my sons' friends over to our house, sleepovers weren't my thing. Come nighttime, I always wanted a little peace and quiet. If there was a long-distance friend or someone who needed to stay over for a compelling reason such as he had no electricity at his house, I was fine with it. But generally, sleepovers were a hard no.

A little desperate, I started to wonder which parts of motherhood I excelled at. My friend, the one who would spend days in the car to glimpse one of her kids, told me I do Shabbat (Jewish Sabbath) dinner every week. While it's true I always spent Fridays preparing for a nice dinner, I didn't think that qualified as good mommying.

I racked my brains. I even thought of asking my sons, but as they can be pretty harsh, I thought better of it. They probably wouldn't have responded to my text anyway.

Then I remembered: I loved to teach them things. I loved cuddling in bed with them and reading to them. Books, poetry, whatever. I was determined to make them literate and literary and, to varying degrees, I did.

I spent gazillions of hours helping them with homework, teaching them their first notes on the piano, discussing world events, etc. When my oldest son made it into the finals of a state vocabulary bee, I coached him with enthusiasm even Knute Rockne would have been proud of. I also loved taking them into the city to see shows, shop, or just walk the High Line. I always tried to support them in the things that mattered to them. I showed up all the time. To the school Halloween parade, to all their band concerts, and to most of their sporting events (even though I don't really like sports).

That's the thing with being a parent. We can't be good at all of it. Some parents love to take their kids on trips or build things with them. Others want to ski or golf with their kids.

But IT DOESN'T ACTUALLY MATTER what you enjoy doing with your kids. There's no need for guilt if you aren't a certain type of parent. Because we all have something to offer. And if it's offered with love, IT IS ENOUGH.

THE HAIRCUT KISS

I often joke about how boys are so different from girls, a fact which is undeniable. Living in an all-male household has given me an opportunity to study how they think and communicate, sort of like what Jane Goodall did with chimpanzees.

After nearly three decades of mothering I can say with all certainty that boys feel every bit as deeply as girls and perhaps are even more nostalgic.

Case in point: the haircut kiss.

Back when my boys were little, and I would take them for a haircut, they would get a "haircut kiss" from me. I was always amazed at how much less they looked like babies after a haircut, and I think the kisses made us both feel better.

As my sons got older, they squirmed a bit when I gave them those haircut kisses but for the most part, they tolerated them fairly well. They probably sensed there was no use resisting. In addition to the kisses, I would tell them how handsome they looked (which off course they did). My youngest son hated getting haircuts, so I only forced him to get one every once in a while. Truth be told, I loved his unruly blond curls and winced a little when I saw them on the linoleum floor. Nowadays, this youngest son of mine likes his hair short and goes for haircuts quite often; sadly, those curls are a thing of the past.

When my sons became old enough to take money from my wallet and drive themselves for their haircuts, a curious thing happened. As soon as they got home, they would find me and offer me their cheek for their kiss and wait to be told how handsome they looked. Of course, I was only too happy to oblige. I would smile to myself, thinking my little boys were in these young men and I was touched that they wanted to keep our tradition going.

(Side note: over the years some of the haircuts my sons got were a little, shall we say, odd. However, unless I was completely appalled, I stuck to the script.)

Since my sons have moved out and gone off on their own, I generally no longer get to see them after they get a haircut, but if they happen to mention it, I send them a text with a kiss emoji.

The other day, I was FaceTiming with my middle son who is working remotely from Michigan. I noticed that his hair looked shorter, so I asked him if he'd gotten a haircut. He said "yes" and then pointed to his cheek for a remote kiss. I gladly threw one to him and told him how handsome he looked.

I have no doubt my sons will remember those haircut kisses for the rest of their lives and perhaps someday offer them to their own children.

I'VE BECOME THE TOWN CRIER

Ever since my sons moved out of the house I have become the town crier.

Whenever there is news to share, I hop on my computer or smart phone and text or email them the latest. I let them know who is getting married, who is going to grad school, who invented a new app and is funding it through Kickstarter. Sometimes (and I hate this part) I inform them of bad things such as an illness, divorce or death.

Occasionally, the news is a front-page type of bulletin —a friend's son got signed by the Boston Red Sox!—but more frequently, my reports are pretty trivial, such as the closing of the frozen yogurt shop or grilled cheese place in town. More often than not, especially when it comes to their peers, my sons (being light years ahead of me on social media) already know what's up. (I'm still working with a string and tin cans while they use technology I've barely heard of.)

I am often a day late and a dollar short on the scoop but that doesn't stop me from trying again and again. I can immediately tell if I've hit pay dirt and managed to impart fresh info by the alacrity with which they respond and their follow-up questions. And here's the part they may not know; I am not sharing news because I am a busybody or gossip monger. My intention is to simply keep them connected to me and the life they have started moving beyond.

I'm glad that my sons are still mildly interested in the happenings in our town and within our immediate and extended family. I must confess to a degree of selfishness in my motives—I want them to know what's going on in *my* world and to remain part of the community in which they grew up. I also admit that, with sons, it's good to have a conversation starter since I'm unlikely (*"highly unlikely"* according to my husband) to talk about their teams' injured pitchers or their fantasy leagues and I can only ask how work/school is and inquire about their health so many times in a week. Local and family tidings seem to be a good way to initiate a conversation.

I will even let you in on a secret—if I have more than one thing to convey I sometimes hold back to have a reason to text them another time. Why report a cousin's pregnancy *and* a town scandal when I can parse out the info? Hey, a mom's got to do what a mom's got to do.

I thought my oldest son might be humoring me by pretending to act interested in my bulletins but when asked, he said he found *some* of my communiqués "helpful" and liked staying current so he knew what was going on when he came home. However, lest I get overly excited and think I was doing something *too* positive or constructive, he added that at times my updates were "inane" and compared them to "talking about the weather." Recently, after I shared a few sad stories in a row, including the death of a beloved neighbor and their middle school principal as well as a classmate's illness, he temporarily suspended my right to deliver news briefings. I was reduced to texting memes I got from the internet and jokes I got from Alexa, (Why did the banker quit his job? He lost interest.)

My middle son, who tends to cut me a little more slack, was more effusive and said he *"loved* being kept in the loop and staying connected." He also pointed out that my husband's mother still calls to keep her 60-year-old son apprised of gossip she hears regarding family, old friends and his hometown, even though he hasn't lived there in 40 years and *she* doesn't even live there anymore. I'm still considering how I feel about being told I've turned into the prior generation.

My youngest son seldom responds but I know he's out there, paying attention in his own way. When asked, he said "It's fine" that I text him updates. A man of few words.

Although the bond I share with my children transcends bulletins and updates, it's likely I will continue to call and text tidbits I deem newsworthy (or at least slightly interesting). In fact, I think I will let them know that someone they know just had a baby.

SON'S GIRLFRIEND: THE BIG MISTAKE YOU NEED TO AVOID

The other day I ran into the mother of my middle son's former girlfriend. Our kids, who started dating in high school, broke up at the beginning of their sophomore year in college. Our encounter wasn't awkward, and I was glad to see her and hear how her daughter was doing; when the daughter was my son's girlfriend, I enjoyed her company.

I have a friend who told me that until a ring is offered and accepted, I shouldn't get too attached to the young women my boys are dating. I'd heard this advice from other people as well. While that may be good advice, it's much harder to do than to say—at least it is for me.

Perhaps it's because I don't have any daughters that I love when my boys bring home their significant others. The entire atmosphere in the house changes when there are girls here. I get to learn about the new fads and fashions in which my boys have no interest or clue. I hear what the girls have been up to, as well as news about my boys and their friends that I might otherwise never know. My oldest son's girlfriend recently told me that one of his good friends had gotten engaged a few months earlier, a bit of information my son didn't think worthy of mention.

When my son's girlfriend visited us shortly after they had attended a wedding, she told me about a website where you can rent dresses. Who knew? (I'm guessing all you moms of daughters knew, but I certainly did not.) I asked my son how the wedding was, and he said "fine." I asked his girlfriend the same question and she gave me a litany of specifics like how many people attended and how the food was. I don't think my boys are withholding details on purpose; they just don't see the relevance in relaying such trivialities. After living in a household with minimally communicative males, these morsels of information are like sips of water to a person who's been wandering in the desert.

After my oldest son first started dating his girlfriend, he told me, "You're going to like her too much and it's going to be a problem." I'm not entirely sure what he meant but I'm guessing he knew I would get attached.

When my sons' girlfriends are around, I get to see a side of my boys I normally don't see. The "young and in love" thing is really sweet—it's good to know my boys can be considerate and silly and tender, different from the rougher versions I typically observe. I have been fortunate because I like the girls my boys have chosen to date thus far. They have been smart, kind, caring, family-oriented, and unspoiled. They are young women with excellent characters, and I'm happy to know my boys have such good taste.

I also have been gratified to see that my sons' girlfriends are amenable to spending time with us. They have been particularly good about including my youngest son when they go out to places like dinner and the movies and have even attended his school concerts and soccer games. My middle son's former girlfriend often helped my youngest with his homework and projects. I once walked in to find her doing his homework while he was nowhere to be found. (I was like "Um, no.")

My sons' girlfriends have been present at holiday meals and celebratory dinners, and spent more than one New Year's Eve with us. They remember to text me on my birthday and offered me comfort when my father died, attending his funeral and shiva (mourning period after). They have encouraged me with my writing career; my oldest son's girlfriend even made me business cards. How awesome is that?

So how in the world am I supposed NOT to get attached? How do other people not get attached? How do they distance themselves from these terrific young women who become (perhaps temporarily) part of the family? Is there some sort of guidebook or manual for this that I don't know about? (After all, I didn't know about the dress rental thing.) Do I really have to wait until they are engaged or married before I get attached? What if they get married and later get divorced? Isn't it all just a moment in time?

After my middle son and his girlfriend broke up, even though I knew that the reasons for their breakup were sound ones and they parted as friends, I found myself missing her. I know that I only had myself to blame because I had broken the cardinal rule by getting attached.

I decided that my friends who told me to hold off until things were "official" before getting attached had the right idea. I thought I'd learned my lesson and I was determined that the next time I was going to play it cool. But then...

My son met a girl during his junior year at college and we had a chance to meet her when we visited him at school last year. A few months ago he brought her home for a weekend so we could get to know each other better. As I spent more time with her, I could see what he loved about her and how much they cared about each other. Despite my best intentions, when I saw how happy he was, I started warming to her. I just couldn't help it.

I admit that I'm just not good at keeping people I like at arm's length. I really don't know how other people do it. I find it hard to imagine that my feelings towards these young women would change the moment after a marriage proposal. My emotions are not like a light switch that I can easily flip on and off.

Another friend of mine is fond of saying "You are who you are" (as you can see, my friends offer a lot of advice) and maybe she is right. I guess what matters most is that my sons want me to know their girlfriends and they feel comfortable bringing them home. And if getting at least somewhat attached is the price I pay, then I'm okay with that.

Update: Since I wrote this piece, which was originally published in *Grown and Flown*, my oldest son did offer a ring which was accepted and, in the summer of 2020, he and his fiancée got married in my backyard. Middle son and his girlfriend also now are engaged—a wedding date has not yet been set. And my youngest also has a girlfriend and yeah, I've gotten attached.

THE MACHATUNIM (IN-LAWS)

Last summer my middlest son got engaged. It was beautiful and romantic and he and my almost daughter fit together like peas and carrots.

But this post isn't about that or them.

This is the second time I've had a son get engaged. My oldest son proposed three years ago and, as I mentioned in the first chapter, got married in the summer of 2020 during the first wave of the pandemic (which was a book in and of itself). The minute the happy couple returned to New York (after the proposal in St. Louis at the school where they met), we had a celebratory dinner with my new daughter's family.

After my middle son's proposal, which took place in Michigan, we had the chance to get to know his fiancée's family. We'd met her sister before, but not her parents. Actually, we went to college with her dad but only my husband remembers him, and vaguely at that.

It's an odd thing to become connected with another family all at once. One minute you're basically strangers, and the next you're kind of related; the Yiddish word for the relationship is machatunim.

Now, truth be told, not everyone gets along with their machatunim. Because it's likely these people are different from you. They do things differently, have different traditions, etc. For example, my daughter-in-law's family are really into fitness. They go for a run on Thanksgiving morning while we lay on the couch and watch the parade which, in my opinion, is much more American. But we like these un-American people anyway.

Maybe your machatunim have different politics or worship differently. There can be a zillion reasons for you not to get along or like each other. Plus, you now have to share your kid and sharing can be hard. Just ask any two-year-old, or parent whose kids aren't coming home for a holiday.

My almost daughter's parents could not have been more kind and welcoming when we met them. My middle son was concerned that perhaps we wouldn't hit it off. I think all couples worry before their parents meet for the first time; it's only natural.

But here's the thing. These people, the machatunim, belong to the person your child loves. And they raised that person. They must have done something right.

And so you look at the things you have in common. Like the fact that you all want your kids to live happily ever after.

My almost daughter said that after the proposal, in the wee hours of the morning, she saw her dad sitting on the couch. And when she asked him what he was doing, he said he was just so happy. He was sitting there being happy. How could we not love this guy?

I am grateful my sons have families who have welcomed them—and us—so graciously.

WEDDING ALBUM

I admit that I dragged my feet signing off on the wedding album my daughter-in-law put together. (Yes, I know the wedding was a while ago—please don't judge.) I thought I looked a little chubby and tired and wasn't eager to revisit the images.

Last night I finally opened the pdf she had sent me weeks (months?) ago and saw a picture I hadn't noticed before. I guess there were so many amazing pictures of my son and daughter's pandemic backyard wedding that I missed a few.

This photo was of my husband and me giving our son a blessing before he and his bride said their vows.

I found myself very moved by the shot.

Our hands are on our son's bowed head, and I am whispering something to him.

I don't remember exactly what I said. But I am certain my words included a wish for good health for him and his wife. As well as all the other things all parents hope for their children on their wedding day. Adventures and love, patience with one another, good fortune, etc. I may or may not have thrown something in about them having kids—I mean it was *my* blessing.

The camera captured a moment I had forgotten. Which is why we have photographers at important events.

I didn't see a tired, chubby me. I just saw love between a parent and child. I am going to try and remember that photo the next time I don't want my picture taken because I'm not happy with my appearance.

GROUNDHOG DAY

We typically mail out our family's holiday card at the end of January and no, it's not late. Our tradition is to send out a card for Groundhog Day. We started doing this a number of years ago because it took the pressure off getting it done when we are super busy in December, plus people seem to appreciate receiving a different kind of holiday card.

In any event, this year both my oldest son's wife as well as my middle son's fiancée are on the card. This is the fifth year the former has been on it and the third for the latter. The first time we considered including the girls they were not yet engaged to our sons, or even thinking about getting engaged. But since they had been together for a while, it didn't seem totally out of line.

I didn't know how to broach the subject with them. It was kind of like asking someone on a date. What if they said "No"? What if they didn't like us well enough to be part of our family tradition? Could I handle the rejection? What if they thought we were insane for sending out a card which celebrated a rodent and a movie (we just love *Groundhog Day* with Bill Murray). What if their parents didn't like the idea? Would they be insulted if we *didn't* include her? Stressful, right?

We discussed it as a family and then I nervously approached them. As I recall, my oldest son's then-girlfriend agreed but seemed a little equivocal to me. When I asked her about it recently, she said that she remembered feeling that it seemed like a big step but that she was "honored." I do remember she helped us design the card that year. My middle son's fiancée agreed quite readily.

Both times we added someone, friends took notice of the additional person on our card, and it didn't take long for them to start asking questions. Like ten seconds after they received it. I told them that there was nothing to report but that they would be the first to know when/if there was official news. Two years after that first girlfriend-included card was sent out, my oldest son and his girlfriend did indeed get engaged.

I have looked carefully at other people's cards to see what they do in terms of significant others.

Some seem to wait until there's a ring on a finger to put a significant other on the card. Some wait until marriage. There was one card that only had the original kids on the front—a new spouse was relegated to the back of the card. It didn't seem like an indictment of the spouse's character; there was even a wedding picture. I guess they just wanted to keep the front of the card as it's always been.

There doesn't seem to be a right or wrong way to do things. There's no holiday card book of etiquette—or if there is, I couldn't find it when I Googled it. (Yes, I Googled it.) I guess if the worst happens and the couple breaks up, they won't be on the following year's card. It's not the biggest tragedy.

Groundhog Day is about a day that is repeated over and over. Life is a lot more fluid than that, and I'm glad that our card reflects the changes in our family from year to year.

WHAT THEY WILL REMEMBER

A decade or so ago, when my boys were ten, fifteen and nineteen, my husband and I took our family to Budapest, Hungary for a vacation.

It was only the second time I had been to Europe, but this trip was important to me because my dad had grown up in Budapest. Plus, I still had family there; cousins and a great aunt whom I wanted to visit.

I'm not a great traveler and taking a journey with my three sons was never easy. But I felt like we needed to do this; I always wished that my father had taken me.

One of the highlights of the trip for me was taking a boat ride down the Danube River. I held my great aunt's hand while we took in the sights—Buda on one side of the river and Pest on the other side. Johann Strauss' waltz, *The Blue Danube*, was even playing in the background. It was a truly magical and memorable afternoon. Or so I thought.

A few months later, I attended my youngest son's band concert and, much to my delight, they played *The Blue Danube*. I mentioned to my son what a coincidence it was that he had learned that song.

"Why?" he asked.

"Um, because you were just on the Danube River."

"I was? When?"

At this point, I'm starting to wonder if he'd had some sort of brain injury I didn't know about.

"When we went to Hungary. Remember, we were on a BOAT????? With our relatives?"

"OHHHHHHH. Was that when you let me have the Sprite?"

Seriously???? I schlepped my kids all the way to Hungary and all he remembered was that I let him have a SODA???? I didn't know whether to laugh or cry. Or both.

I must believe he absorbed more than that from the trip.

That's the thing with memories. You never know what will stick and what won't.

I imagine that many of us grown-ups won't remember the pandemic too fondly.

But who knows what our kids will remember? Maybe they will think some of it was amazing. Zoom calls with relatives. And Thanksgiving in our pajamas, or outside. Or lots of family time and doing puzzles. Or something seemingly insignificant like a Sprite.

As I've indicated in previous anecdotes, our household was not always a calm one. In fact, quite often it was the opposite. There was a lot of commotion and yelling. I've mentioned that my older sons were a little high strung. And I didn't always have the patience I needed.

Many years ago, after a particularly bad day, I said to my oldest son that I feared that all he and his brothers would remember of their childhoods was the yelling. To which he immediately replied, "Nah, I'm going to remember that we laughed our asses off." I hope so.

Only time will tell.

IT'S NOT US, IT'S THEM

Our kids think we are weird, but we know the truth; it's them not us. And for all you parents out there who are still in the thick of parenting, don't let them try and convince you otherwise.

For years, I listened to my boys talk about how other parents were more normal/better/cooler/less annoying than I was. And on occasion, they made me doubt myself. It was hard not to. So and so's mom let him stay up as late as he wanted. XY and Z's parents didn't care about their grades. Everyone else's parents let them underage drink and have parties. Why, oh why, did they have to have the misfortune of having me as their warden/mom?

As hard as it was, at the risk of my own mental health, I stayed the course. I parented in the way that I thought was in their best interests. I always told them that if I made mistakes, it was not out of selfishness or laziness. At least I was always there, front and center. Every band concert, every Halloween parade, every everything. Okay, maybe I missed some soccer games, but that was largely my husband's department.

Yes, OF COURSE I made mistakes. Not a single parent since the dawn of time has NOT made mistakes. That's not even a thing. I can guarantee that Adam and Eve made mistakes. Although at least their kids couldn't compare them to other parents.

If I could do it over, I would have done some things differently. I would have worried less about the college thing. I would have worried less in general. Because I learned that they change/get less weird/figure it out as they grow up. I would have been a laid-back mom instead of an uptight mom. Okay, who am I kidding? I would have been the same mom because that's who I am. My name is Marlene and I'm a neurotic mother.

In any event, for anyone out there whose kids are complaining about them, never mind. I'm here to tell you that, if you are trying, you are doing a fabulous job. Trying counts for a lot. If you are off somewhere ignoring your kids, well, that's another story. I mean, good for you and please send me a postcard, but you're not winning a Parenting of the Year award.

In the end, I'm happy I was true to myself as a parent. And now that they are grown, maybe, just maybe, my kids are happy about it too.

THE WORRYING NEVER ENDS

My oldest son, who is 30, wasn't feeling well. And when I texted him to see how he was doing he said, "You don't need to worry about me."

Bwahaha.

Apparently, he doesn't know how the system works.

Basically it goes like this: Our kids are born and we start worrying. Actually, we start worrying even before they are born.

And it never ends. NEVER. Not when they are 10 or 20 or 30 years, 6 months and 8 days old. Dinosaur moms probably worried about their 300-year-old dinosaur children.

We worry when they go to nursery school and kindergarten and college. We worry when they are sick or unhappy. We worry when they don't text us back. We worry they might get their hearts broken. We worry when there's a pandemic and when there's no pandemic. We worry that they might be cold or hungry. And on and on and on.

So my dear son, it's super nice of you to tell me that I don't have to worry about you. But until I take my last breath on this earth, I will be your mom. Which means I will worry.

P.S. If there's an afterlife, I will worry from there too.

HOW IT STARTED, HOW IT'S GOING

My older two sons didn't always get along when they were younger. Although my oldest son desperately wanted a younger brother, when one finally arrived on the scene, he wasn't quite sure about the situation.

Although he wasn't always patient or kind, I knew my son loved his brother. One time, when my husband and I went out for an evening and left the two of them with a babysitter, we came home to find them in bed together. They had watched a Planet of the Apes movie, which scared my younger son—he kept saying, "Where's the happy ending?" So my older son decided he needed to keep him company until we got home which was sweet. But there were many times when things weren't so loving between them.

Their complicated relationship came to a head when my middle son was fifteenish and my older son was 19 during that trip to Hungary. We were with cousins when my oldest son said or did something my middle son didn't like. It dawned on him that he was now bigger than his older brother and he unleashed a lot of hurt and testosterone – basically they had a brawl in a pastry shop. It wasn't pretty. They had another fight months later in the backseat of our car – punching each other from the window seats with my youngest son in between them. Again, not pretty.

Things settled down between the two of them. They grew up. And my oldest son became the mensch we always hoped he'd be.

My oldest son and his wife bought a two-family house in Brooklyn, and they just moved in.

They offered the first-floor rental apartment to my middle son and his fiancée and told them they were welcome to use the rest of the house, as well. The engaged couple happily accepted.

My kids will be living together again. Because they want to. I don't know how it's going to go, but the fact that they are even trying it is not something I could have imagined a few decades ago.

You can do everything right and your kids might not like each other. Sometimes that's just the way it goes.

But if you're lucky, you will have kids who choose to be a part of each other's lives. And that's a pretty incredible thing.

Move-in day in Brooklyn

MOM-1-1

Mom-1-1 What is your emergency?
Can you send my suit? I have formal coming up.

Mom-1-1 What is your emergency?
Can you text me the recipe for the chicken I like?

Mom-1-1 What is your emergency?
Would you be able to come to our house inspection on Monday?

Mom-1-1 What is your emergency?
Can you find out if I had a tetanus shot?

Mom-1-1 What is your emergency?
Can you help me pick out an engagement ring?

Yes, these have all been actual requests from my adult children. I don't really answer my phone or texts by saying "Mom-1-1 What is your emergency?" However, I do feel like I'm on call.

That's what it's like having grown kids. Although we are no longer driving carpools, watching soccer practice, or helping with homework, we still are very much parenting. No, not all the time or in the same way, but we are there, waiting to be summoned. Like the people who answer the 9-1-1 calls.

I enjoy being needed some of the time. It gives me a chance to still do things for my kids while having time to do things for myself as well. Things I didn't get to do when I was full-time mommying.

And since I also don't have the energy or the stamina I once did, (which honestly wasn't that much to begin with) a part-time gig is perfect.

> Mom-1-1 What is your emergency?
> None, I just called to say hi.

Yeah, sometimes I get those too.

Life is good.

Making me laugh so
hard that I pee in
my pants isn't the
accomplishment it
once was.

~Thoughts From Aisle 4

2. WE AREN'T GETTING ANY YOUNGER

WE'RE NOT AS YOUNG AS WE USED TO BE

I started thinking about how there are certain things we do when we become, shall we say, not as young as we used to be. A kind of how-you-know-you're-not-25-or-even-35-anymore list.

Here are a few of the things I thought of:

- You can't remember where you parked your car. And if you happen to be driving a different car (loaner, spouse's, kid's), there's virtually no chance you're going to find it. You might want to just walk home or call an Uber.

- There are physical therapy exercises you should be doing while you're watching TV. For your back, knees, shoulder, you name it. Sometimes for several body parts at once!

- You want grandkids before you completely fall apart.

- You repeat the same stories—over and over. But luckily so does your best friend, so it's okay.

- You call your kids by the wrong names, including the dog's. Actually, I've always done that, so never mind.

- A first-floor master bedroom, or primary bedroom as it's now called, sounds like the greatest idea since sliced bread.

- You wonder what the hell is wrong with most people.

- You'd rather stay home than go out. And if you go out, you'd like to be home by nine or ten at the latest.

- A day when nothing hurts is like all the stars aligning.

- You have doctors' appointments for different body parts at least every month. By the way, don't forget to schedule your mammogram, colonoscopy, ophthalmologist, dermatologist, annual physical, gynecologist, dentist, etc. And each doctor you see is likely to require follow-up for something or a new medication. A good day is when you scuttle out of a doctor's office with an "all clear until next year."

- You're trying to figure out where you want to live when you retire. This is a big topic of conversation among middle-aged people. There are those who want to move somewhere warm and then the anti-Floridians who hate humidity and shudder at the idea of living there.

- You've taken up pickleball. And canasta and possibly mah-jongg.

- You need stronger reading glasses. Again.

- Your circle of friends has gotten smaller but closer.

- You own a seven-day pill holder.

- Getting a good night's sleep is something you brag about. And you're happy if you only got up to pee once during the night.

- You want to get rid of all the excess crap in your house.

- Having little kids seems like a lifetime ago, even though each day raising them felt like an eternity.

- Your days and years are not dictated by the school calendar.

- A cup of coffee with a friend or a non-complaining phone call from one of your kids is enough to make your day.

- You are wiser, more tired, crankier, and grateful. Grateful things aren't worse and grateful for all the good things in your life.

I may be a little grayer and shorter than I used to be and I need glasses to read anything smaller than a stop sign, but the good news is...damn, I have no idea what I was going to say.

~Thoughts From Aisle 4

DECLUTTERING BEFORE YOU DIE

A recent hot new craze is the Swedish custom of decluttering before you die known as *dostadning*. I am not a fan.

Don't get me wrong, I love new trends. I was the first one in for mood rings and pet rocks and my kids had all the Beanie Babies and Webkinz. Anyone who knows me knows how obsessed I am with *hygge*, the Danish art of coziness. In fact, as I type this, I am under a blanket and have a candle burning nearby. For the record, I found the book about tidying up by Marie Kondo helpful, if not life changing. But this new Swedish thing is where I draw the line in the sand.

The concept behind this Swedish custom is that you start getting rid of things before you die so that your kids don't have to go through your stuff and be burdened with the task. They recommend beginning at age 50 and really kicking things into high gear at 65. Well, I am 58 and I am just not ready to start paring down. I still have a kid in college, for goodness' sake. Yes, I realize I'm not a spring chicken, and my left hip has been hurting for years, but I don't see any buzzards circling overhead, thank you very much.

When my husband and I first got married, and for many years after, we had to be quite careful about spending money because we had a ton of school loans and didn't have much for extras. Then the kids came along, and we had to start saving for their college educations and such. So now that we are finally in a better financial situation, we have to start winding things down?? What happened to the time in the middle when we could buy what WE want?

And let's get back to talking about those kids. I refuse to worry about what my kids will have to do after I'm dead. I have spent three decades devoting my entire existence to them. I honestly don't care about making their lives easier after I'm gone. There are three of them—they can figure it out or hire someone to do it for them. I am not going to worry that something I am buying will make their lives more difficult. In fact, some of the crap in this house is theirs and they seem to be in no hurry to get rid of it.

My mother-in-law recently downsized, and when she was in the process of packing, I told her that she should get rid of stuff so that she could fit into her new place. Now I feel badly about giving her that advice—who was I to tell her how to live her life? She's earned the right to do whatever she wants.

They are trying to sell this death cleaning thing as a positive and happy experience, but I'm not buying it. Any trend with the word death in it isn't for me.

I'm not saying I want to become a hoarder; being somewhat mindful of what we purchase is not necessarily a bad thing. However, I am not going to look at something and say, "maybe I shouldn't buy this because I'll be dead soon and it will have to be disposed of." Hell no. In fact, I think I will go do some online shopping right now. There's a new bag I've been eyeing for a while.

A MESSAGE FOR THE OVER FIFTY CROWD

I woke up yesterday morning after having slept eight and a half consecutive hours. This is significant because I generally spend some time in the middle of the night staring up at the ceiling contemplating life or, if I get really desperate, reading for a while until I can go back to sleep.

But two nights ago that didn't happen; I didn't even get up to go to the bathroom. Upon opening my eyes I was startled by a few things—first, I wasn't tired because I had slept pretty well. Second, *nothing hurt.*

Now some of you hearty younger people reading this probably are a little confused and are saying to yourselves, "Why is that a big deal?" Well, I am of an age that when nothing hurts, it's noteworthy. Like take-an-ad-in-the-newspaper or write-a-blog-about-it noteworthy.

A friend of mine, who is the same age as I am, told me that when she wakes up, she takes inventory of her body to see what her health status is. She said she does this before she even gets out of bed, so she knows what's up. I totally knew what she meant. I have a chronic lower back and left hip issue. Despite doing my stretches and special exercises, I can only expect to feel so spry on any given day. I wouldn't want to jump out of bed (even if I could jump) before doing a thorough assessment—it could be dangerous.

I plod through most days aware of my body's reminders that I am no longer twenty. Or even thirty. My hands shake, my knees make a popping sound when I stand, I can barely see things right in front of me without my reading glasses, and everything is starting to droop. There are the headaches, which come and go, and the ever-present fatigue. Most days, if I sit down for more than a few moments in the latter part of the afternoon, there's a good chance I will doze off.

It seems like everyone I know who is about my age has a litany of aches and pains as well. If I had a dime for everyone who has a shoulder problem, carpal tunnel syndrome, arthritis, high blood pressure, high cholesterol, etc., I'd be rich enough to pay my health premiums and then some. A good friend just herniated a disk in her back lifting a *bag of toiletries*. She was indignant that the bag wasn't even heavy. But that's how it goes these days.

When I'm with my peers, our conversations are often peppered with words like "procedures, appointments and follow-up." Let's face it, peeps, we are getting to the point where our bodies are showing wear and tear. We're not quite ready for the junkyard, but we are certainly well past the new car smell. Maintenance of ourselves is becoming more and more time consuming. If I could get an extended warranty on myself, I would.

The good news is we are living in a time when medicine is getting better and better at repairing us. My husband just had laser eye surgery for a tear in his retina, which is fairly routine as are things like knee and hip replacements.

I am well aware that these are all small problems and, although they can be annoying and even disconcerting at times, things could be a whole lot worse. *I truly am grateful* to still be here, and I accept my body for what it is; appreciative that it has gotten me this far.

Today I was back to my usual tired state of being, having been awake from 2-4 a.m. Although I was a tad disappointed, I couldn't string two great days together, I can't say I was surprised.

My plan for the future is to enjoy the terrific days, accept the sub-par ones and muddle through the bad ones. I guess it's the best any of us can do.

TRAPPED IN MY SPORTS BRA: A HARROWING TALE—PART ONE

A few months ago, I put on a sports bra—the kind that goes over your head, not the kind that hooks in the back. It was a little snug because it was old, and perhaps it had shrunk. Okay fine, maybe I had gained a few pounds.

Anyway, after my workout I went to take off my bra. But I was still sweaty. Any woman who has ever tried to get a tight spandexy item off her body (think wet bathing suit) can probably guess what happened next.

It got stuck.

So there I was, trying to contort my body, pulling and tugging, trying to get the bra over my head. And it wasn't working. Obviously, I couldn't call for help. "Hello, 911 what's your emergency?" "Um, I'm trapped in my sports bra." No. Just no.

A little panicked, I started thinking of other options. Maybe I could find a pair of scissors and cut it off. Or I could just stand there for the rest of my life, in my bathroom, with a sports bra somewhere between my boobs and my neck, contemplating the life choices which had gotten me there.

Eventually, I got the d*#n thing off. I think I worked off more calories trying to extricate myself from the bra than I had on the treadmill earlier.

However, in my desperate attempt to pull the bra over my head, I did something to my left shoulder. That was months ago and my shoulder still hurts. From taking off a bra. Now I can barely take off a t-shirt. I know that it will eventually heal, but this was honestly just a ridiculous way to injure oneself. I will not go to a doctor because I will not humiliate myself even further by explaining how it happened.

Who did I think I was, trying to shimmy out of spandex at my age? This was another cruel reminder that I am no longer twenty.. Or even forty.

You'll be happy to learn that I threw out those too tight bras and replaced them with bras that hook in the back.

I've learned my lesson.

I will never again endeavor a physical feat which should only be attempted by young nubile gymnasts.

I tell you my bra tale of woe, not for sympathy, but as a cautionary tale. If I can save one person from injuring themself, then my pain will have been worth it.

TRAPPED IN MY SPORTS BRA: A HARROWING TALE—PART TWO

I figured I'd give it time. I'm at the age where my body heals slowly. Actually, I'm at the age where my body does everything slowly.

But after six months, I'd finally had enough. So I went to the orthopedist my husband had seen when he hurt his shoulder several years ago. At our age, shoulder injuries are right up there with creaky knees and hips.

The person who did my intake was a guy. And when he asked me how the injury occurred and I told him about the sports bra, he totally didn't get it. Blank stare.

Luckily, the orthopedist was a woman who understood—she even nodded her head in solidarity when I explained how I was held hostage by my bra. And she was wearing nice loafers. I notice these things.

The doctor sent me for an MRI. Literally my worst nightmare.

I drove myself to the MRI and, on the way there, it dawned on me what I was in for.

The panic attack started as soon as I saw the MRI machine, which is a long tube. Not good for anyone who is even mildly claustrophobic. And I am majorly claustrophobic. Like I don't go into caves. I don't even love elevators.

I realized I should have taken something to calm me down. I thought about rescheduling, but I was already there and didn't want to have to go back.

I couldn't use the headphones they gave me. I took off my mask. I declined the blanket they offered. I couldn't have anything on me. And even still, I felt like I was suffocating.

I tried closing my eyes and thinking about the ocean. The clanging of the machine made any thoughts impossible. I sobbed. I asked to stop a few times and they obliged, rolling me back out so I could breathe. I explained that tight spaces were my least favorite thing in the world. I imagine I wasn't the first to freak out.

In any event, I powered through the ordeal and after what felt like an eternity, I was done.

Good news: nothing was torn. I merely had a frozen shoulder. Apparently it's a pretty common thing. Especially after a certain age. "After a certain age" is my new catchall phrase by the way. Like in "After a certain age, there's risk involved in asking your body to do anything it did when it was younger."

I got a steroid shot and then started physical therapy; after several weeks, my shoulder started to defrost. No big deal. Could have been so much worse.

I feel like I learned a bunch of valuable lessons:

- Don't wear things that are too tight.

- Don't wait forever to check out an injury.

- Find a good physical therapist and be super nice to them because, going forward, you're going to need them.

On a positive note, the whole shoulder episode gave me the title of my second book—*Trapped in My Sports Bra and Other Harrowing Tales*. I'm hoping it will be a bestseller.

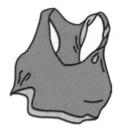

3. THANK YOU FOR THE MUSIC

PHISH AT THE BEACH

*T*here we were, minding our own business and relaxing in a cabana by the beach on the first day of our vacation when we heard a guy in the next cabana over, which was practically on top of us, playing guitar.

At first, I was a little annoyed because I hadn't slept well the night before and really wanted to nap, but I had to admit the guy was pretty good. He was working on a country song, apologized, and said he was going to sing a mermaid song with his ten-year-old daughter after her friends finished burying her in the sand.

He and his daughter harmonized so beautifully that I asked if he were a professional, to which he replied "no" but was certain his daughter would be some day. I told him he had perfect pitch and he demurred and again praised his daughter. I then asked if he ever recorded anything, and he gave a vague "no" but did say he's played with "some bands."

Since he seemed to like country music, I may or may not have asked him if he sang any John Denver songs. We talked about some of his favorite artists who had inspired him. He and his family, along with friends that were with him then went off to the water, which he didn't think was going to work out well because the water temperature was chilly.

I then trotted off to the restroom, as I seem to do a lot these days, and left my husband to gather our things. I was waiting for him to meet me, but he didn't show. I checked my phone to see he had texted our eldest son and me. "Trey is HERE!" he exclaimed, to which our son quickly responded "Yeah right" in complete disbelief.

I know my husband. This was no false sighting. So I ran to where he was and asked, "Where is he?" and my husband pointed him out. Since I know Trey only by name, I asked my husband how he knew it was him. He told me he walked by while Trey was talking with the couple with whom he was still conversing and overheard him say that "they had just performed in Boston at Fenway." So I asked how he knew that "they" just played Fenway and he told me a friend had posted on Facebook from the Boston concert.

"They" are Phish and "they" are what our oldest son does when he's not working. He's seen them play 54 times —he's known of their existence for maybe 13 years. That's a lot of concerts in a lifetime, let alone a little over a decade.

So I did what any mom would do, and I approached the ginger-haired guy and asked, "Are you Trey Anastasio?" He could not have been nicer and said that he was. I explained that I knew of him through my son and, although I didn't know what any of the Phish members looked like, I knew they "were old like me." Again, I have to say how incredibly gracious Trey was. I told him how a few months back, while my husband and I were in Florida, we had received an alarming phone call from our youngest son saying he had been "kidnapped" by our oldest and was being transported against his will and across state lines to a Trey Anastasio concert and was being forced to break Passover with pizza during the car ride to the concert.

Trey seemed to find the story amusing and asked where we lived, what my husband and I did for a living and, since the conversation was going well, I again did what any mother would do—I asked if he would agree to talk on the phone to our son, who was at work. Trey quickly agreed and, as soon as our son answered, Trey said, "Hi, Eric. It's Trey."

Our boy tried to play it cool with his idol on the other end of the phone, but I knew he was DYING. They chatted for a few minutes and Trey told our son that he was on his side in the whole kidnapping episode. It then dawned on me that our next-door cabana mate was another member of Phish, as was the guy two cabanas over. There was a whole school of them!

Trey encouraged us to go tell the kidnapping story to the guitar-playing next-door neighbor (who my husband now was able to identify as Mike Gordon) because he thought he'd appreciate the Passover part. My husband said to Mike, "You lied to us about being a professional musician," to which Mike said, "I didn't lie; I withheld information." Hmmmm.

Now that I know how talented these guys are and how nice they are as well, I'm thinking I may go to one of their concerts. By the way, this won me MAJOR mom points with my son.

MY FIRST PHISH CONCERT

Meeting three of the four members of Phish in person motivated me to go to my first Phish concert. When we bought the tickets, I didn't realize that we'd be seeing them at the end of Thanksgiving weekend and that there would be crappy weather. But hey, few things in life are ideal, right? And if you can't go with the flow, you probably shouldn't be going to a Phish concert.

So, we met up with my oldest son and his wife for dinner and then we all drove over to Nassau Coliseum on Long Island.

Right off the bat, I have to say that the guys in the band are great musicians. I kind of already knew that from getting a personal concert from Mike Gordon. I really do appreciate good musicianship. In addition, although I have no idea what their relationships are like in real-life, on stage Trey, Mike, Page and Jon are a well-oiled machine. They look to each other for signals, especially Mike and Trey, and you can tell that they share a language and a certain kind of chemistry that only people who have been together forever can share. It's like being an old married couple.

I was a little surprised that the band members don't really interact or speak with the audience when they perform. I guess they want their music to do all the talking and tell the stories for them.

About their audience—wow. Just wow. Trey had told my husband and me that there is an awesome Phish community, but you have to experience it to really understand it. The people there were just so nice. And polite. And considerate. But most of all, they were happy.

Like my son, they knew which song was about to be played before they heard the second note, and they knew every word to the songs that had words. I had never seen so much dancing at a concert. People moving their arms and bodies and swaying like they do in a gospel church. Which I suppose Phish is to many people.

One thing I didn't love is the smoke. I'm a bit sensitive to smoke and there was a lot of it. I don't really care what anyone is smoking; however I don't love to breathe it in. The people around me were more than happy to share what they were smoking, but I politely declined. Much to my son's amusement, I got offered acid, which he said was not a usual occurrence, but again, I just said "no." The person who offered it to me really didn't know how totally square I am. Like think of the squarest person you know and then sharpen those edges even more.

I made a few new friends, including Chris, aka "Dobby," who told me he thought the show was around his 500th and another new friend who gave me a sparkly bracelet in honor of my first concert. I enjoyed the vibe around me and loved seeing people so joyful. There isn't enough of that these days.

As a side note, when I had to use the bathroom, I was DELIGHTED to discover that the line to the men's room was about a mile long, while the line to the women's bathroom was almost nonexistent. My daughter-in-law said that's how it always is at Phish concerts. I hate to break things down to such a basic level, but bathrooms are important to me. If nothing else, Phish had me at the bathroom situation.

The only song I really knew was *Avinu Malkenu*, a Jewish prayer chanted on the High Holidays, which I LOVED. Apparently, they rarely perform it, and it was a real treat to hear it live. My husband and I left before the end and I missed the other song I knew, *Backwards Down the Number Line*, which made me a little sad. But I guess it gives me a reason to go to another concert.

One of the things I enjoyed most about my first Phish concert was sharing the experience with my son and his wife. As my kids have gotten older, like most parents, I sometimes struggle to connect with them. I don't love sports, which is a big part of my sons' lives, so I was grateful that I was able to see one of them in his happiest place, being himself.

Did I love it? Yeah, I guess I did. I may never get to 500 shows, but I'm glad I got to one.

I THINK I LOVE YOU—MY CRUSH ON DAVID CASSIDY

I got a text from my cousin that David Cassidy was in a coma with organ failure. The news really stopped me in my tracks. Celebrity deaths happen every day, and many of them make me pause—especially the ones who remind me of my youth, like Michael Jackson, George Michael, etc. I think about their music, or movies that they were in, and feel nostalgic for talent lost and bygone days.

But the news that David Cassidy was critically ill made me particularly sad. He was my first and biggest crush. There were others of course: Bobby Sherman, Donny Osmond. But no one was David.

I know he was not just *my* first love. When I posted a picture of David and me on Facebook from when I saw him (and his brother Shaun) in the show *Blood Brothers* on Broadway almost three decades ago and said he was in the hospital in critical condition, there was an instantaneous response from many women my age who were as upset as I was.

They commented that posters of him had adorned the walls of their childhood rooms. I'm still getting comments and private messages about how much he meant to them—personal recollections and anecdotes. We feel a kinship with one another, a bond that's hard to explain.

There just was something about David. He had the smile, the charm, the voice and, of course, the hair. He wore his puka shell necklace and bell bottom jeans with confidence.

I looked forward to Friday nights and *The Partridge Family* all week. Even though David's character Keith was not as cool as he was, when he sang, his charismatic persona shone through and I was completely captivated. I knew every word to every song on those Partridge Family albums and sang along lustily, using my hairbrush as my microphone.

I knew that David's favorite color was green, his birthday was April 12 and his favorite song was *The Thrill is Gone* by B.B. King. I read everything about him in *Tiger Beat* magazine and imagined I was his girlfriend. There have been many other teen idols since David, of course, but none as big. None have even come close. He was lightning in a bottle.

Long after I grew up, his music could still make my heart flutter and remind me of some of the nicest moments of my childhood. After I saw him in his show on Broadway, I waited outside the theater door to meet him. He started to walk away but my husband yelled out that it was my thirtieth birthday. So David graciously came back and wished me a happy birthday and we posed for a picture. We didn't have a camera with us, so a lovely couple from England snapped that photo and took my address. Months later, long after I had ceased thinking about it, the photo came in the mail. There was no return address on the envelope, so I couldn't thank them, but their kind act meant a tremendous amount to me. (If this piece somehow makes it to you in England, I am forever in your debt.)

I saw David perform in person again years later, and I was once more reminded how talented he was. David had had his share of personal struggles, but his voice was still strong and sure. During that concert, he sang many of the songs from *The Partridge Family*, as well as others. Even though we were both now much older, I was instantly transported back to my youth. He seemed to embrace what he was to a generation of women who fell in love with him so many decades earlier and, although he probably didn't understand it (because who really could), he seemed to appreciate that some of the old feelings remained.

In recent years, I had read about his failing health, which included alcoholism and dementia. I felt sorry that, despite his talent and fame, his life was such a difficult one. I listened to many of those old songs after hearing the news and still knew all the words.

Thank you, David, for the music, the fun, and for being my first love.

4. GONE, BUT NEVER FORGOTTEN

FOR ANYONE WHO HAS LOST A SIBLING

I sometimes have specific questions about my childhood. But there's no one I can ask or with whom I can reminisce because my brother, who was my only sibling, died in 2008, when he was 48 years old.

When my brother and I were children and we would fight, my mother would say to me, "You only have one brother; you have to get along." As an only child my mom had no firsthand knowledge of sibling rivalry. She wanted nothing more than for us to be close.

My brother was four years older than I was and as a child that seemed like a lot. We shared a bedroom in our little house in Brooklyn and had bunk beds; my brother had the top bunk, and I was down below. I had an earlier bedtime than he did but if I was still awake when he came into our room we would chat for a bit. Sometimes he would lean over the side of his top bunk and reach down so that we could engage in a thumb war.

Back then we often got on each other's nerves, as siblings do. It didn't help that my brother and I were different in a lot of ways. He loved to be outside in the winter while I loved to be inside. He had a lot of energy; I was more sedentary. He was quiet; I was chatty. I wanted to be left alone to read and he wanted to do stuff. Like all the time.

When we moved from Brooklyn to a bigger house on Long Island, we finally had our own rooms, which were located next to each other. Although I loved having my own space, I sometimes missed having him right there. Before we went to sleep my brother would knock on the wall between our rooms and I would knock back. We had our own special code. Like the thumb wars, it made me feel less alone.

As we got older, I realized that we had more in common than I had thought when we were kids. The four-year age gap and differences I had perceived as important when we were younger became less significant when we became adults. We started our own families and celebrated holidays together, and we grew closer. I admired the passion with which he lived his life and the joy he found in traveling, skiing, playing tennis, and so many other things.

Sometimes a week or even two would go by without us speaking on the phone but then we were always happy to catch up. I always knew he was there for me, and it was a comforting feeling. When I had appendicitis and was stuck in the hospital for more than a week, he closed his dental practice in New Hampshire and came to New York to hang out with me in my hospital room and play cards. I was grateful for his company.

When I took my family up to visit his, my brother would take my babies out of my arms to help me. He was gentle and kind to my boys— he taught my oldest son to water ski and always seemed happy to have them around.

His death devastated my sister-in-law and their sons, leaving a gaping hole in their lives. My family lost something as well and it makes me sad that my boys didn't know him longer. I am positive that my brother would have been extremely proud of the men my two nephews, who were teenagers when he died, have become. He would have been happy to see them in solid relationships and successful in their careers. And he would have been over the moon thrilled by his grandson. He missed out on so much.

Around the time my brother got sick, my father was diagnosed with Parkinson's disease. My brother was smart and patient and I had counted on him to be there to help with decisions regarding our parents and their health care. I hated being thrust into the role of only child. When my father passed away, I gave the eulogy on behalf of my brother and myself; I tried to include the things I thought he would've wanted me to say, and I felt his presence as our father was laid to rest.

I visited my brother in the hospital shortly after he was diagnosed with brain cancer and had started treatment. When I saw him lying in his hospital bed, I hid my anguish and told him to move over, so I could get into bed with him. I made him laugh when I told him I needed to rest more than he did, but I think he knew I wanted to be next to him so that he would feel less alone, just as he had always made *me* feel less alone.

Before he died, he told me I was a good sister and I told him he was a good brother; we left nothing unsaid. However, it would've been okay if we had not spoken those words because we both knew how we felt.

Siblings are the people who sometimes defend and frequently torment you when you are young (anyone remember something called an Indian rope burn?). They are also the ones who corroborate your memories and comfort you when you are older.

My mother was right, I only had one brother. And I miss him every day.

REMEMBERING MY DAD

On Father's Day, my family will be celebrating my husband, who is an amazing father. But I will also be thinking about my father, who passed away six years ago.

A little about my dad...

My father was born in Budapest, Hungary in 1932. When the Nazis invaded Hungary in 1944, both his parents were taken to Auschwitz. He was interned in a ghetto and lived with an aunt and a cousin, surviving under the protection of Swedish diplomat Raoul Wallenberg. His mother escaped during a death march, running away into the woods, and hiding in a barn, eventually returning to Hungary. His father died at Auschwitz in the gas chambers.

My dad emigrated to Canada after the war ended with a group of Hungarian teens who had lost parents in the war—his mother eventually emigrated there as well. He attended McGill University, met my mom who was visiting relatives in Montreal, and moved to New York when they married. He worked as an engineer and was able to get his master's degree from Columbia University at night.

Although the Holocaust certainly shaped my father, he tried hard not to let it define him and rarely spoke of the atrocities he witnessed. He made sure to live life fully, enjoying good food, wine, and music. He was quick to laugh, especially at his own brand of dad humor. My father embraced his adopted country and was deeply grateful for the freedoms and opportunities afforded him here.

Having been born in different countries and in different eras, my father and I saw things from different perspectives. He was a staunch Republican, whereas I am a liberal Democrat. When I was a little girl, he would take me into the voting booth with him and tell me about the importance of voting and how lucky we were to live in a democracy. I always vote and when I choose my candidates, I think of him.

Although I thought of my father as a math/science guy, he was also more than proficient in writing. In fact, he was able to edit my essays in high school and correct my grammar. Impressive for someone whose first language was not English. He was my first Scrabble opponent and he never went easy on me. Although it took me two years to beat him, when I finally did, he was as excited as I was.

Despite losing his own father at a young age, my dad knew how to be a good father. He taught my brother and me how to ride a bike, fish, ice skate, swim, and play chess, which was a passion of his. He got up in the middle of the night with me when I was sick and dried my tears when I cried; he couldn't bear to see me sad. He taught me a lot about nurturing and made me feel safe. When he held me in the ocean when I was a little girl, I knew I would be protected against the crashing waves.

My father was thrilled to become a grandfather and delighted to be able to attend all five of his grandsons' bar mitzvahs. Although he was mostly confined to a wheelchair for my youngest son's bar mitzvah, he did manage to get up so that he could have one dance with me.

When he got sick with Parkinson's disease, he rarely complained, accepting his fate with quiet grace and even humor. In fact, a few days before he died, a nurse asked him if he was comfortable, to which he replied, "I make a living." And even in such a compromised state, he managed to chuckle.

I would be remiss if I didn't mention my father's thriftiness, which was legendary. If saving money were an Olympic sport, he would've been a gold medalist. He would turn off the air conditioner on summer nights and turn down the heat in the winter. To this day, when I leave a light on, I can hear his admonishment in my head. And every time I spend four dollars on my iced coffee, I am pretty sure he does a little roll in his grave.

I suppose that's how it is with all the people we love. We never forget them or the things they taught us. We are reminded of them in the special moments and in the ordinary moments. They live on through the people they loved and who loved them back.

Happy Father's Day to all the dads who are with us and to those who live on in our hearts.

MY FATHER'S GLASSES

After my father died, my mom asked me what she should do with his eyeglasses. I investigated the matter and found a place that accepted donations and brought my dad's glasses there. I put them all in the bin and walked away. And then I went back and took one pair out and brought them home.

It should be known that I am not a hoarder. In fact, as of late, I love throwing things out. Purging is my new favorite sport and when I see a dumpster in front of someone's house, I get envious.

But I just could not get rid of every single pair of my father's glasses. Even though they were going to a good cause, I needed to save one.

My dad started wearing glasses when he was in elementary school, and I rarely saw him without them; he pretty much only took them off to rub his eyes or when he was going to sleep. His eyesight was bad and got progressively worse as he got older. In fact, in his seventies he went blind in one eye.

His glasses were really thick, the proverbial coke bottles. When I was a child and would occasionally put them on, I was amazed at how blurry they made the world and was grateful I didn't need to wear them to see clearly.

My dad wore the type of frames that had been in style in the seventies, but he could not be convinced to update them. That was typical of my father—he had his own way of doing things and his own sense of style. And let me just say he was not a fashion icon; for decades he wore a green track suit that my husband still jokes about. He wasn't much of a shopper but when he did decide to buy clothing, the discount store was his favorite.

When from time to time I open the case and look at the glasses I instantly see my father in their reflection. And I know that's why I saved them. We don't necessarily need *things* to remember the people we love, but sometimes an object can be such an integral part of a person's physical being that it's too hard to part with it.

I'm glad I saved those glasses.

WHAT TO EXPECT WHEN YOU'VE LOST YOUR BABY

This is for anyone who has lost their baby, through miscarriage, stillbirth, or infant death. I want to speak directly to you because I am one of you, decades into the future. I want you to know what you can expect, sort of like a *What to Expect When You're No Longer Expecting, and Your Baby is Gone* guide.

As I mentioned in an earlier chapter, I lost my first son to a congenital heart defect when I was twenty-six years old, and he was ten days old. He was born by Cesarean section four days after my due date, after a placental abruption, and weighed in at 8 pounds 14 ounces. Sonograms were less sophisticated than they are today, and his heart defect was not detected on the one sonogram I had. When I went into labor, I was completely unaware of how my life was about to change, which I guess pretty much sums up most catastrophes which befall us.

After his death, there was the heartbreaking funeral with his tiny casket and subsequent mourning period. But what happened after that?

Thankfully, there was no baby stuff to return because, although we had picked stuff out to be delivered after we brought our baby home, none of it was in our apartment other than a car seat. In the Jewish tradition baby showers are not allowed—it's a superstition I fully support.

The obstetrician who delivered my son, and who was a wonderful and caring person, assured me that after I had more children, the death of my first son would merely be a footnote in my life. And while I did go on to have three more beautiful and healthy sons, I can unequivocally state that he was incorrect. My son's death changed me in profound ways and taught me a lot of lessons. I learned that people don't always deal with death well, especially those who have not yet experienced a loss themselves. For many people it's easier to offer platitudes or even avoid a difficult topic altogether than to confront their own discomfort. Most of my twenty-something friends were not yet in an emotional position to help me.

Comfort may come from unexpected and even surprising sources. My husband and I joined a support group full of strangers who had experienced similar losses. By sharing our heartache we started to heal.

I learned that the only important outcome of a pregnancy is a healthy child, not the manner in which they are born nor their gender. I learned that, although you will be forever changed by your baby's death, life goes on. And that there will be joy in your life again.

If you want to have more children, you will. And I don't say that lightly. I do not have a crystal ball regarding your fertility, but I do know that if your desire to have another child is strong enough, your baby's death won't stop you (as you know, I went on to have both biological and adopted children). If you don't want more children, there are other ways to nurture. I have friends who were involved in raising their nieces and nephews.

You will never forget your baby's birthday, or their death day, and you will always be acutely aware of all the milestones they will never experience. However, you will have a richer and deeper appreciation for things others take for granted. This deeper appreciation is a gift bestowed upon you by your baby and one only you and your sisters-and-brothers-in-grief can understand. On the surface, you will appear to "have gotten over it" or "have moved on", but unless you are able to erase your memory like they do in those *Men in Black* movies your experience and sorrow will alter you in ways you cannot imagine right now but that are surprisingly positive and affirming.

The sadness, grief, shock, anger, and bewilderment you are feeling right now will ease. But long after most people have forgotten your baby ever existed, even decades later, you will be able to remember exactly how you felt when you had to say that excruciating goodbye. Thirty-two years later you will still cry when you think about him and then, as you wipe your tears away, you will see that the sun is shining as you close your computer and start the rest of your day.

In Memory of Jared...

FROM BEYOND THE GRAVE

I know a woman who is a medium. That's not her size, it's what she does. Meaning she can speak to the departed.

When I was younger, I would've said that isn't a thing. But I've experienced some unexplainable events, plus I feel like I've gotten more open-minded as I've gotten older.

I tried to imagine myself doing a session with her so that I could communicate with some of my dead relatives. But the more I consider it, the less I think I should.

Let's start with my dad (may his memory be for a blessing). As I've mentioned, he was one of the most frugal people I've ever known. If he wanted to get in touch with me, he'd find a way to contact me directly—there's no way he would speak through an intermediary who charged by the hour. In fact, if I did hire her, he'd probably be so angry that he wouldn't speak to either of us.

Although of course it would be nice to hear my dad say "I love you" one more time, I know it well enough. Honestly, there really isn't much for him to say to me, unless he had some secret bank account somewhere in which case I'd really like to know. Maybe I can try a Ouija board instead.

Then there's my brother (may his memory also be for a blessing). He would probably tell me to be more patient with our mom. To which I would reply, "Easy for you to say since you're dead and I'm here." I guess I should cut him some slack because dying wasn't in his grand plan. I suppose he has a point and I *could* work on being a little more patient.

I think our loved ones wouldn't want us to feel too sad about their deaths or badly about things we think we could have done differently. (What if I noticed their symptoms sooner? What if I had chosen a different doctor or treatment plan?) When you love someone you want them to be happy, right?

After I'm gone, I do not want my kids to try and contact me. Not that they would. They barely call now (see how I threw in a little Jewish guilt there?). Plus they know that I would just nag them: "Why didn't you wear a warmer jacket? I noticed you haven't had a green vegetable for over a week. When was the last time you had a haircut?" And so on. It's not like the grave is likely to stop me from voicing my opinion.

I'm making sure to say everything I need to while I'm still here. So that in the event of my untimely passing my kids know my thoughts and hear my voice in their heads.

Actually, I'm pretty sure they already do.

5. LAUGHTER REALLY IS THE BEST MEDICINE

BREAKING NEWS: FRATERNITY CAUGHT FORCING PLEDGES TO READ MOMMY BLOG

*A*s part of a bizarre initiation ritual, a fraternity at a university near Boston, Massachusetts has been caught forcing its pledges to read a mom blog. The blog, which is written by a mother of one of the fraternity brothers, focuses on parenting and middle-age issues.

The alleged hazing came to light when one of the pledges cracked under the stress of being made to read the blogs and a book the mom had written about her oldest son's backyard pandemic wedding. He reported the fraternity to the school's administration for "cruel and unusual practices."

The student, who wished to remain anonymous to avoid retribution, said, "At first, it wasn't so bad, and I even chuckled when I read some of the pieces. But then it got to be too much. The last straw was having to read a piece about menopause. I was like WTF. After that I was out of there. I honestly would have preferred to swallow a goldfish." He added that, "Instead of joining a frat, I've decided to become a member of the quidditch club."

The University Administration announced it would investigate the matter. An administrator in charge of Greek Life said that, "If the allegations are true, there could be serious consequences and we may have to punish the fraternity. No student should be subjected to this kind of treatment. However, on a personal note we are all really enjoying the blogs and can't wait to read more of this woman's stuff. She's funny. We can't wait for her next piece, and we are hoping she writes another book."

The son of the blogger, who is a junior at the university, stated that he was "only trying to help" his mother. He said that the student who reported the fraternity probably wasn't "brother material anyway" and next time they would be more careful with their initiation practices.

Further details will be reported as they occur.

MOM STILL CONFUSED ABOUT OFFSIDE RULE AFTER 25 YEARS OF WATCHING HER KIDS PLAY SOCCER

At her son's soccer game earlier today, a local mom was struck by the realization that she *still* didn't completely understand the offside rule in soccer.

The mother of three sons, who did not want to be identified so as not to embarrass her family, said that although the rule had been explained to her countless times, she didn't fully get it.

When asked what she thought the offside rule is, the mom said that she believed it had to do with "someone being in front of someone on one of the teams when they shouldn't be because the ball is someplace else." Although her answer was correct in a sort of roundabout way, it in no way really explained anything.

The mother said she began attending her sons' soccer games nearly 25 years ago, when her oldest began playing the sport in nursery school. Since then, all three of her boys played soccer on various teams, including in high school, college, law school, and even in an adult league on weekends. In addition, the woman stated that her husband and sons are all certified referees and watch soccer on the weekends, with each of them supporting different teams (Go Arsenal, Manchester United and Everton!)

She acknowledged that she should have "learned more about the game after being exposed to it so much" and couldn't comprehend why she found it so difficult to understand the offside rule. She thought that it might have something to do with the fact she tended to "zone out" every time she saw people "running up and down the field." She admitted that during the games she found herself thinking about a lot of other things and often chatted with teammates' parents.

On a positive note, the woman said she now had the ability to open one of those collapsible chairs with the cup holders in the arms in under five seconds and get it back in the bag in ten, as well as cut orange slices like a fruit ninja.

With her youngest son entering his senior year of high school, the mom vowed that by the time he graduated, she would not only understand the offside rule but would also be able to teach it to other confused parents.

We'll check back with her in a year and keep you posted.

BREAKING NEWS: WOMAN BLASTED FOR WEARING CASUAL ATTIRE TO BACK-TO-SCHOOL NIGHT

A local woman was heavily criticized for wearing unstylish clothing to back-to-school night at her daughter's high school a few days ago. The woman, who did not wish to be identified, said she realized she was garnering stares as she walked from class to class but was unsure why.

A close friend pulled her aside after fourth period and explained that she should have given more thought to her appearance for the social outing. The woman said she had been so busy feeding her children dinner and trying to tidy up the kitchen that she had forgotten to even change into a clean shirt before rushing to the school. She said she had felt pleased she'd remembered to brush her teeth.

Having been initially focused on her child's curriculum, after her friend spoke to her, the woman looked around and saw that most of the other mothers were dressed as if they were attending a fashion week runway show. Many women wore skinny jeans and peasant blouses and teetered in the  hallways on five-inch wedge heel strappy sandals. Unfortunately, as they ran class to class a few toppled over but were quite graceful as they fell.

She also noted most of the women seemed to have had their hair blown out, fresh manicures and professionally applied make-up. Feeling a little ashamed and self-conscious, the woman tried to cover the macaroni and cheese stain on her t-shirt. Another mother in attendance said that the ill-dressed woman was "setting a bad example which could affect the district's state ranking."

Chastened by her faux pas, the woman resolved to do better at her son's back to school night at the middle school the following week. She said she planned a trip to the mall for a new outfit and handbag and was blocking out the entire afternoon to get ready.

Further details will be reported as they occur.

LOCAL MAN SHOCKED BY DNA RESULTS

A local resident has been rocked to his core by the results of a DNA test. After receiving the findings of his *23 and Me* analysis in the mail, the man, who wished to only be identified as "Buddy," discovered that he is 15 percent canine.

Buddy said that when he did the DNA test, he was fairly certain that it would show he was exclusively of British and Irish descent. In fact, he stated that "I would have been surprised to find that I had French and German or other Western European ancestry, never mind canine."

Buddy's wife said that the results "explained a lot of things," such as her husband's "tendency to shed a lot of hair in the spring, his keen sense of smell plus his desire to retrieve things." She also revealed that he loved to have his tummy rubbed, often had "sudden bursts of energy" when he would dash around the house, and was eager to get the newspaper every morning, waiting by the window for its arrival. She stated that although the information didn't change her feelings about her husband, it made her realize that "no one can really know their heritage without scientific evidence."

In addition to his Anglo and canine ancestry, the DNA results showed that Buddy was two percent Native American, as well as five percent Sardinian, both of which he found even more surprising than his canine roots. When interviewed for this article, Buddy stated, "It would take some time to process the information." He cautioned that before doing one of the genetic kits, people should be prepared for shocking revelations, although he conceded, "They might find relief in learning why they exhibited certain behavioral quirks, such as having a fondness for balls or getting excited when cars go by."

Further details will be reported as they occur.

**Nothing says
"I love you"
like not asking
what's for dinner.**

~Thoughts From Aisle 4

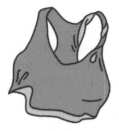

6. LOVE AND MARRIAGE

> "To love and be loved is to feel the sun from both sides."
>
> —David Viscott

FRIDAY FLOWERS

*L*ast Friday my husband came home from work with a bouquet of flowers: coral-colored roses which are my favorite.  It wasn't my birthday or our wedding or dating anniversary, he wasn't bringing them home as an apology or a peace offering after a fight. He brought them home because that's what he has done every week for the past 40-plus years.

My husband and I met on my first day of college. I was not yet 18 and he was 20. We dated for almost six years before we married; this August we will celebrate our 35th wedding anniversary. It's hard to believe we've been together for more than two-thirds of my life.

When we were in college my husband started buying me flowers that were sold in the student union on Fridays. The flowers cost one dollar for three carnations of assorted colors and, even though my husband was on a tight budget and had no money for extras, he presented me with those flowers week after week. Even when we were mad at each other about something he bought me those three carnations, which I put in an empty wine bottle because I had no vase, and I always thanked him with a kiss.

The flowers are representative of the man my husband is and one of the reasons I thought we could be a good fit for one another. I had a very short list when it came to choosing a partner, but I was not willing to compromise on any of the things on that list. I wanted someone who was kind, traditional and intelligent. The rest was up for grabs.

I figured if I found someone who was those three things, we would have a good shot at a happy life. I had seen plenty of marriages that had dissolved or were fraught with discord to know to look for qualities that would stand the test of time. I am now old enough to understand that there is also a component of luck involved in staying happily married. People change, people give up on each other. Sometimes people give up on themselves and are so unhappy that they simply cannot be there for anyone else. But even back then I knew that a person who is kind is likely to remain kind; the essence of a person doesn't change.

My husband shows his kindness in countless small ways rather than with grand gestures. When he returns from work, he always asks me if I need anything before he eats his dinner and is happy to make me a cup of tea when I request one. He remembers to pick up my favorite magazine when he passes a newsstand, always replaces the toilet paper roll (he's better at that than I am), checks in with me when he has a free moment at work, and is supportive and encouraging. Several years ago, when I went through a rough patch emotionally he was there for me in every way.

The two of us have weathered a lot, which I realize most people do if they are married longenough. However, our marriage was tested early on by the loss of our infant son. Although we were both so young, we learned how to lean on each other while still allowing space so that we could grieve individually. Over time the losses added up, my beloved brother, both our fathers.

My husband spent long hours at the office building a career and with the addition of each child the little time we had for each other diminished further.

I was often left to parent our three high energy sons by myself, a job I frequently found lonely and exhausting. Occasionally I imagined a life back in Boston working at my old job and I suppose he had his own fantasies. There were nights we went to sleep angry at each other, which I'd heard you weren't supposed to do if you wanted a happy marriage. We probably broke other rules on the how-to-stay-happily-married list as well. But we always managed to find our way back to each other. He has exhibited the steadfastness I saw early in our relationship, and I knew he was not one to give up on us.

The flowers my husband brings me now cost much more than a dollar and are much more exotic than those carnations, but the meaning behind them has stayed the same. Even if we're angry with each other, even when we haven't brought our best selves to our marriage, the flowers represent the commitment we made to each other and continue to make week after week.

I'm not saying that weekly flowers are the key to a happy marriage. In fact, I don't believe there is one recipe for a happy marriage because no two marriages are the same. But if you remain resolute and recall why you chose one another back at the start, the good times will outweigh the bad. Each week, in fact *each day*, is a chance to look back and remember and then look ahead and recommit.

And to my husband: thank you for all the flowers and I love you.

MY 13-WORD MODERN LOVE STORY

A few years back, *The New York Times* had a contest where they asked their readers to submit 13-word love stories for their *Modern Love* section. The rules for content were pretty open—marriage advice, how you met, etc. I was delighted when I received an email saying that I was one of the winners and that my submission had been selected to appear in the paper—beating out ten thousand other entries! Here is what I came up with:

Never bring up similarities between
your spouse and your mother-in-law during a
fight
~Marlene Fischer, Westchester, N.Y.

[*The New York Times* Editor's note: we are treating mother-in-law as one word here, because we couldn't resist]

Now I certainly know that every couple is different, and there isn't one recipe for success; however, this advice certainly can't hurt. But since I no longer have a word limit there are a few other things I'd like to add.

It's important to fight fair. In addition to not bringing up similarities between your spouse and your mother-in-law during an argument, don't talk about past digressions. Keep the discussion about the here and now and keep the disagreement constructive. As I mentioned before, I think it's okay to go to bed mad sometimes, but I also think it's important not to let fights go on too long.

Work on bathroom etiquette. Flush, replace the toilet paper roll (yes honey, I know I forget to do that sometimes), cover the toothpaste tube, wipe around the sink, etc. A few small things can say to your spouse, "I care that you are not grossed out or inconvenienced when you enter the bathroom." No one likes to reach for toilet paper and find it's not there. 'Nuff said.

Stay off your devices. This one can be tough. With work and social obligations and those darn funny memes, our phones and other devices can be addictive. Carve out a little time to BE with each other without the distraction of electronics. That tiny device can create an incredibly large wedge between you.

COMPROMISE, COMPROMISE, COMPROMISE. In a marriage no one gets their way all the time. That's not how it works. When my husband and I got married, he liked Crest and I liked Colgate. SOOO, we decided to use Colgate every day and Crest when we travel. Another example—he was a Mets fan, and I was a Yankees fan. Our kids are all Mets fans, and I gave up on baseball. I caved on this one because it was way more important to him that it was to me. Choose the things that matter most to you and let the other things slide. You come from different homes with different traditions; you can't pass down everything.

Be kind. They say a little kindness goes a long way and it's true. If your partner is sick, make them tea and bring them soup. If they seem sad, cheer them up! It can be tough out there in the world. It's up to you to bring a little compassion and understanding into your spouse's life.

Encourage each other. Be a one-person cheering section. Nothing says "I love you." more than "You can do it." or "I believe in you."

Laugh. A little bit of humor makes everything better. What do you call a fake noodle? An Impasta!

And last but not least:

When the going gets rough, remember all the reasons you chose one another in the first place. There will be rough patches; that is a guarantee. Life is capricious and sometimes even cruel. But together, you can get through those rough patches.

No two marriages are the same, and everyone must figure out what works for them. But being kind, having respect for one another, caring about the other person at least as much as you care about yourself, listening, hearing, and being able to laugh together are certainly a good start.

A REALLY EXCELLENT PIECE OF MARRIAGE ADVICE

I was watching a television show not too long ago when I heard a piece of marital advice that I thought was good. In fact, it was more than good, it was surprisingly sage and sensible.

The show I was watching was *Blackish* which, in case you haven't seen it, is a comedy/drama about the Johnsons, an affluent suburban family. The Johnson family consists of the parents Rainbow (Bow) and Andre (Dre), five kids ranging from baby to young adult, and a set of opinionated grandparents who also live with them. I honestly didn't love the show when it began, but it found its groove and got much better after the first season, so I stuck with it.

During one season, Bow and Dre begin having some serious issues with their marriage. Their normal bickering morphs into open hostilities. The addition of their last child, as well as health issues and other life stressors put tremendous strain on their marriage.

The fighting was depressingly real with Bow and Dre rehashing old arguments and dealing with new resentments and I considered dropping the show from my weekly watch list. Although I thought the show was interesting and informative and gave an important perspective on Black life in America, I didn't tune in to see constant quarreling. I found it uncomfortable and disheartening.

Bow and Andre decided they had had enough and chose to separate, with Andre even moving out and getting his own place. But then (spoiler alert here) Bow's father died, and she reached out to Andre who came home to comfort her. And then he stayed after both of them realized they wanted to be together.

In an effort to work on things they went to a marriage counselor who gave them that excellent piece of marriage advice I mentioned earlier. She told them that marriage is like Thanksgiving dinner. The marriage is the turkey; you season it and stick it in the oven and then you start working on the sides. The sides are everything else: jobs, children, house, vacations, etc. And while you're dealing with all that other stuff, you forget about the turkey, and it starts to burn.

It's an analogy and message I really could relate to. My husband and I have been married for close to thirty-five years and we have come close to burning the turkey many times. The "sides" in our lives often felt as if they were taking precedence over the turkey. Although we only have three and not five children like Bow and Dre, the ten-year age gap between our youngest and oldest, as well as their strong personalities, often made it feel as if we had more than three kids around here. Quite frankly, they were a lot to handle. Add in my husband's job, which was more like two full-time jobs, and all the other things which life entails, and there really wasn't a lot of turkey time. In fact, there were times I barely could remember where the oven was, never mind basting and checking on that bird.

One would think that as our kids have gotten older, we would no longer need to worry about finding time for each other. But that's the thing; you can always find other stuff to do. You must make your marriage a priority. It needs to be "checked on." If two people don't want turkey or hate Thanksgiving no amount of basting that bird is going to help. However, if you are both into making a great feast, you can make it happen.

You never know where an important kernel of advice might come from. I was surprised to get marriage guidance from a television sitcom but glad that I tuned in and paid attention. So yeah, work on the cranberry relish, candied yams, and pumpkin pie, but don't forget to look in the oven every now and again, because the whole meal really does depend on it.

IT'S NOT ABOUT THE RING

I occasionally see a Facebook status from a newly engaged young woman where she is beaming and displaying her diamond ring. I really enjoy seeing the happiness and sparkle which radiates from both the bride-to-be and the ring. I admit I also like seeing the different shapes of the diamonds and settings they are in; I'm a sucker for romance and all things shiny. I am also reminded of my own engagement and proposal which occurred over 37 years ago and came with a card instead of a diamond.

As I've mentioned, my husband and I met on my first day of college. When we got engaged five years later he was in law school and up to his eyeballs in student loans. We had discussed getting married, but he surprised me by proposing after we'd had dinner at an Italian restaurant in Boston, where we both were living at the time. He actually asked me to marry him after the meal was over, outside the restaurant because he didn't want to do it in front of the people sitting at the table next to us. He was so nervous that he handed me a card with the words he was afraid he might mess up if he tried to say them. The card, which I still have, was very sweet and detailed the reasons he wanted to marry me. I'm not sure why he was so worried; I was kind of a sure thing, although I understand that it was a momentous (and hopefully) once-in-a-lifetime event.

After I said yes, he was very happy and relieved and offered to take out another loan so that we could pick out a diamond ring. I found his offer incredibly sweet and, even though I'd be lying if I said I didn't want a diamond, I declined and said we would figure out something that fit his budget. We eventually chose a small pink sapphire and he told me that someday he would replace it with a diamond.

As the years went on, it seemed as if there was always something more important to spend money on besides a diamond ring, like paying off those student loans, buying a house or car, saving for our sons' education, etc. But eventually, seven years ago, after nearly 27 years of marriage, the time seemed right for such an extravagant purchase. We shopped for the stone together and then I chose a platinum setting I had admired for a while.

A few weeks later, my husband arrived home early from work one day. Unbeknown to me, he had picked up the finished ring.

I was busy getting ready for a holiday, dealing with my middle son who was sick, and completely harried and distracted. My husband seemed nervous and stood in front of me somewhat expectantly. Impatiently I asked, "WHAT?" He then got down on one knee and presented me with the ring. I was surprised and touched.

Once again, I was not sure what he was nervous about because after three kids and decades of marriage, I was *even more* of a sure thing than the first time he proposed. Obviously I said "yes" and he put the ring on my finger. In the midst of the chaos that was our life we reaffirmed the commitment we had made three decades earlier.

The ring has even more meaning to me now than it might have years ago. Back then it would've only been a symbol of things to come; now it represents promises fulfilled as well as the future. When I look at it I am reminded of the two times my husband got down on his knee and asked me to travel the road by his side.

In the end, it's not about the ring. As much as I enjoy seeing it sparkle on my finger, I know that love does not need a symbol to endure, just a commitment between two people, determined to journey through life together.

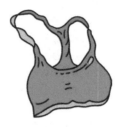

7. POTPOURRI OF ME

I'VE DECIDED TO BECOME AN INSTAGRAM INFLUENCER

I wrote a piece about a jacket that had become so ubiquitous, it was literally impossible to go anywhere without seeing it. Shortly after, a reader sent me an article about an influencer who wore the jacket all the time. A little curious, I checked out this influencer on Instagram. I was surprised to see that this young woman had over a million followers and had gotten so famous, she started her own brand of clothing.

I looked at this woman's pictures of her and her adorable children in their beautiful apartment in Manhattan and decided that I too would like to be an influencer. It seems like a really great job. You get free stuff and people know who you are.

There are a few obstacles with my plan, however, none that I think are in-surmountable.

First, I'm not young. That's okay because instead of influencing the younger crowd, I can influence middle-aged women like myself. Just because we aren't young doesn't mean we can't be adorable. Okay, maybe not adorable but cute. Hmmm, perhaps not cute but sophisticated. I will circle back to deciding what my exact vibe will be.

As for Instagram followers, I already have over 800 which is not that far off from a million. I may need to post more pictures to grow my following. Not a problem. I noticed that the influencer often posts photos of her and her children in bed. I can do that—I love to be in bed! I can take selfies of myself keeping it real with my anti-aging cream, wearing my favorite XXL college sweatshirt —the one that has the holes in it which, I see, is quite fashionable. On second thought, that might not attract potential followers, so I may need to post pictures of me somewhere other than in bed.

Since I don't lead a terribly glamorous life, I am not sure where. The grocery store? Target? Do influencers shop at Target? Will have to research that. As far as clothing, I don't have flowy flower dresses; I tend to wear my comfortable mom jeans. In fact, my favorite jeans actually say Mother on them. Maybe I could be a brand ambassador for them. After raising three sons, I am definitely a mother. And G-d willing, eventually maybe I could start my own line of Grandmother jeans that are even more high waisted than Mother jeans. A girl can dream, right?

I don't have a chic and well-appointed Manhattan apartment, but I do have a comfortable house in Westchester. I've been throwing stuff out Marie Kondo style—I just got rid of a 24-year-old green couch that hasn't brought anyone joy in decades, so the place doesn't look half bad.

Next: the influencer is skinny. Like she hasn't had a cookie in decades. Or pasta. Which is like me, except it's only been a few hours since I've eaten those things. I admit to having a muffin top. Is there a place for an influencer who's a little chunky? This could be a deal breaker because I really do like to eat. Maybe snack companies will send me free stuff. I'm a big fan of dark chocolate and things covered in dark chocolate, in case anyone wants to send me some products to promote. But I'm not that finicky, so whatever you send me is fine.

Children—as I mentioned earlier, the influencer has three adorable little girls. They are so cute you can almost smell their sweetness when you look at pictures of them. I have three grown sons who really don't like to smile for the camera. In fact, to discourage me, my oldest son has made a habit out of snarling when we attempt to take a group picture. Maybe I can borrow someone else's children.

I'm starting to realize that being an influencer could be harder than I thought. If you have any ideas, please let me know.

THE GOLDEN GOOSE (SNEAKERS)

Last year when I was in a consignment shop in my town, I laid eyes upon a pretty pair of sneakers. I liked them. However, when I mentioned to the store owner that she was selling scuffed sneakers, she gave me a look of pity that she probably saves for only the most uninformed. She explained to me that these sneakers were called "Golden Goose" and came dirty right out of the box. Like even the brand-new ones. "Hmmmm" I thought.

Of course, after that, I started to notice Golden Goose sneakers everywhere. You may have seen them too without even realizing what they were. They have stars on the side of them and they are chic sneakers made for chic people. So, as a fast-rising influencer, I went to a specialty retailer to check them out.

There were dozens of styles to choose from. Glittery ones, high tops, different colors. I picked out a basic style and tried them on and waited to feel chic. Except nothing happened. Not only that, but they didn't even feel all that comfortable.

I also felt that for the hefty price tag, they should make me feel more special, like Cinderella in her glass slippers. I thought they looked like a version of Converse sneakers people owned in the '70s—after wearing them in.

I also wasn't quite sure how I felt about pre-scuffed sneakers. On the one hand, sneakers that come with dirt on them would save me the worry and angst when I got them dirty myself. It's sort of like buying a new car that already has a ding on the door. When the next ding happens, you aren't so upset.

On the other hand, was I really willing to pay for dirty footwear (although I do own pre-ripped jeans)? I also tend to shy away from dressing like the herd—would these sneakers make me a conformist?

The Golden Goose is a fable written by the Brothers Grimm about greed; was I supposed to learn a lesson from the sneakers? These were moral questions that gave me a headache as I stood in the shoe department and tried to answer them.

In the end, I decided to pass on the Golden Goose sneakers, although a friend of mine told me she loves them (but only after she changed the insole to make them comfier). I purchased another pair of plain of white sneakers instead. And of course, me being me, tripped the second time I wore them and scuffed the front of one of them and then a week later, scuffed the other one. At least the sneakers matched.

I admit I felt a little bad about it and thought perhaps it was karma for judging the Golden Goose sneakers. My middle son noticed the damage and mentioned that I could get the scratches buffed out; however, I decided that by leaving them I was making my own fashion statement.

So, if you see me walking around town in scuffed white sneakers, I would appreciate it if you could please remember the extreme angst and effort that went into creating this fashion statement and mention how chic I look.

AN INTERVIEW WITH ME

For those of you who don't know me, I thought I'd interview myself so you can get a better sense of who I am.

Me: Why did you name your blog *Thoughts From Aisle 4*?

Also Me: Actually, my oldest son came up with that name based on the voicemail message that's been on my phone forever: "Sorry you missed me, I'm probably in *Aisle 4* at the grocery store—I will call you back when I'm done shopping." And most likely, that's really where I was. I spent a lot of time there when my three boys were growing up and I still do some of my best thinking while figuring out what to make for dinner. My town is lucky to have a wonderful grocery store and I like food shopping.

Me: What is *Aisle 4* about?

Also Me: It's about everything and nothing. Raising three boys, life in the burbs, getting older, becoming a mother-in-law, television shows I'm watching, my constant battle to keep my hair from frizzing, dealing with the pandemic, politics, etc.

Me: Have you ever written anything that hasn't upset at least one person?

Also Me: I wouldn't say never, but rarely. People are touchy, especially lately. At first it really bothered me because who wants to get yelled at? But now, most of it rolls off my back. Because I understand that people are cranky and are dealing with their own stuff.

Me: Do your kids mind you writing about them?

Also Me: No. When I started, I had them read everything I wrote before I put it out there, but then they told me to stop sending my posts to them because they really didn't care. I guess they trust me enough not to tell the most embarrassing stories about them. With my new daughters I've had to be a little more careful, but they don't seem to mind either. In fact, I think they're all a little proud of me and *Aisle 4*. And that feels pretty good.

Me: Where are you from?

Also Me:—The East Coast. Brooklyn NY, Merrick NY, Nashua NH, Waltham, MA, Boston MA, East Rockaway NY, Plainview NY and for the past 24 years, Westchester.

Me: Where are your readers from?

Also Me: I asked them that once and was astounded to discover that I have readers from pretty much EVERYWHERE!!! I know the internet is a global thing but it still blows my mind.

Me: What do you do when you're not in *Aisle 4*?

Also Me: Well, I spend a fair amount of time writing for other publications and editing college essays along with my friend and business partner Helene. It keeps me out of trouble and from shopping for new handbags, which has always been somewhat of a passion of mine. Life is better with a good handbag.

Me: What are your politics?
Also Me: I won't comment on that other than to say I'm a liberal democrat. I'm about fixing the environment, gun control, women's rights, gay rights, working on racism in our society, etc. I think you get the picture. There are plenty of Republicans in *Aisle 4* and they are welcome too—I grew up in a conservative, Fox News watching household, so I know the drill.

Me: Why do you have a blog?
Also Me: I'm a glutton for punishment? I have no idea. I just like to put my thoughts out there I suppose. I'm a writer. It's a creative outlet. Plus, I've met such incredible people here and I'm proud of the *Aisle 4* community. I also hope that people connect to what I'm saying and feel less alone when they read my words.

Me: Are you married?
Also Me: Yes. I've been happily married to Mr. Aisle 4 for 35 years—and we've been together for almost 41 years. He proofreads most of my posts and is very supportive in every way.

Me: Is there anything else you'd like your readers to know?
Also Me: Hmm. Maybe just that I appreciate them. And if there is anything they'd like me to write about they can let me know.

Me: Thanks so much for your time.
Also Me: My pleasure! Thank you for interviewing me.

CONFESSIONS OF A BLOGGER

My name is Marlene, and I am a blogger.

It all started innocently enough with a few blog posts on WordPress. Having always enjoyed writing I figured I would just jot down a few thoughts in between loads of laundry and put them out there. I learned how to set up my site and was up and running in no time at all.

I shared those initial blogs on Facebook and smiled at the likes and encouraging comments I received. I admit that the positive feedback felt good, and I was deeply grateful to the friends who shared my blog posts. I checked my stats and marveled at all the people in the different countries who read my posts. I said things like, "Isn't that lovely, someone from Australia just read my blog!" It was just nice to be writing again. I hadn't realized how much I had missed it.

But all too soon it became apparent that my little WordPress site wasn't going to be enough. I needed more. I moved on to sending out my blogs to online publications. A dear friend, who I now realize was an enabler, had sent me the list to feed my addiction.

When the first blog I sent out was accepted for publication, I felt heady intoxication. Positive reinforcement became something I started to crave. I was used to snarky comments from my children, not this sudden validation that I still had a brain. It was a rush I couldn't explain. I also discovered that the blogging community is one that is composed of supportive and intelligent people. It was a community I wanted to be a part of.

Each day I searched for topics to write about. I lay awake at night thinking about my next blog topic—hoping for an idea that would go viral. Friends and family started to shy away from me, concerned that anything they might say in my presence might turn up in a blog post. "Write about something other than us," my middle son implored. Was there something other than my family I could write about? I considered my son's request for a moment but then realized that I'd spent decades devoting my life to my children and they owed me— it was my right to write about them and their antics. Antics, which, I might add, had probably taken years off my life.

My existence had become so much about being a mom that, when it came time to send a bio and headshot to the online publications, I couldn't even find a picture of myself that didn't include my husband and kids. I finally found one where I was able to mostly crop them out.

In my quest to write the perfect post the laundry started piling up, the breakfast dishes remained on the table, and I stopped going to my spin class. Okay, maybe I hadn't started taking a spin class, but I had definitely considered it. I knew I would have to get myself under control before I lost it all.

I decided that while I would continue to write, I would do it at a more moderate pace. I would allow my family a modicum of privacy and scale back on checking the views and clicks my posts received. I even bought a Peloton bike for the house so I can take classes in between writing gigs.

This is a cautionary tale for anyone considering starting their own blog. Blogging can suck you in before you realize what is happening. Proceed with caution. But if you have a desire to write, do proceed, because it really can be fun and fulfilling.

**I'm pretty sure my kids
conspire with each
other to drive me crazy.
Like in a group text
when they wake up—
"Who's got mom today?"**

~Thoughts From Aisle 4

CONCLUSION

*I*n the Introduction I said that there was no overall theme to this book, that it was just a compilation of random stories. But when I read it through again I realized that wasn't true. I've probably written a thousand blog posts and could have chosen any of them to include. But these stories are not here by happenstance—they are the ones that meant the most to me (except maybe for a few I threw in just for fun.)

We all have incidents and stories in our lives which stand out. Thank you for allowing me to share some of mine with you.

- *A Letter to a Younger Me From an Older Me* and *Remembering My Dad* originally appeared in *Inside Press*

- *This is Why Teens Find Their Moms Annoying* and *Son's Girlfriend The Big Mistake You Need to Avoid* originally appeared in *Grown and Flown*

- *Six Things You Need To Know About Having Grown Sons* originally appeared in *Her View from Home*

- *I Think I Love You, My Crush on David Cassidy* originally appeared in *Huffington Post*

- *A Note From Mom, The Job I Always Wanted, Groundhog Day, I've Become the Town Crier,* and *A Letter to My Sons,* originally appeared in *CollegiateParent*

ABOUT THE AUTHOR

Marlene Kern Fischer is a wife, mom, food shopper extraordinaire, blogger, lifelong writer, and college essay editor. She attended Brandeis University, from which she graduated *cum laude* with a degree in English Literature.

Having survived her kids' pandemic wedding which she chronicled in the best-selling book *Gained a Daughter But Nearly Lost My Mind: How I Planned a Backyard Wedding During a Pandemic*, Marlene decided to write a second book with all of her free, non-wedding planning time.

Marlene lives in Westchester, New York with her husband and dog Maisy. Despite the fact that she writes about them, her kids come home to visit frequently.

You can follow Marlene's blog *Thoughts From Aisle 4* on Facebook or find her on Instagram @aisle4Marlene.